# Christ Crucified

A 21st-Century Missiology of the Cross

Mark W. Thomsen

**Lutheran University Press**
**Minneapolis, Minnesota**

**Christ Crucified:**
**A 21st Century Missiology of the Cross**
by Mark W. Thomsen

Library of Congress Cataloging-in Publication Data

Thomsen, Mark W., 1931
    Christ crucified : a 21st century missiology of the Cross / Mark W. Thomsen
        p.cm.
    Includes bibliographic references
    ISBN 1-932688-01-3 (alk. paper)
        1. Missions—Theory. 2. Jesus Christ—Crucifixion. 3. Suffering—Religious aspects—Lutheran Church. 4. Lutheran Church—Doctrines. I. Title

BV2063.T42 2004
266'.001—dc22

2004043843


Lutheran University Press, PO Box 390759, Minneapolis, MN 55439
Manufactured in the United States of America

# Contents

# Acknowledgments

I thank countless friends and vibrant people encountered—personally or through books—within the worldwide human family, most of whom have been members of the Christian community. They have been witnesses to the power of hope and joy in the midst of the tragic reality of human suffering, to the horrendous chasm between wealth and poverty, to enriching patterns of cultural and religious diversity, and to insightful and powerful dimensions of the Gospel often neglected and dismissed by theologies locked in fortresses of Western orthodoxy and academia.

I wish to thank students at the Lutheran School of Theology (LSTC) who participated in my classes (1997-2003): Jesus within Religious Pluralism, The Theology of the Cross and Religions in Dialogue. Their insights received in discussions and papers are reflected in this volume. I also wish to thank Dr. Vítor Westhelle for the invitation to teach the Theology of the Cross course with him during the spring of 2001. Our discussions and the outstanding group of students in that class were a valuable learning experience for me. My deep thanks also to Dr. Harold Vogelaar, Dr. Ghulam-Haider Aasi (Muslim) and Sensei Seven Ross (Zen Buddhist) for the enriching challenges shared while co-teaching Religions in Dialogue at LSTC.

A number of people read this manuscript and offered valuable evaluations and critiques of the material. Thanks to Dr. Carol LaHurd, Dr. Richard Jensen, Dr. Harold Vogelaar,

Dr. Vitor Westhelle, Dr. Paul Rajashekar, Dr. Paul Sponheim, Dr. Thomas O'Meara, Dr. Winston Persaud, and my second Theology of the Cross class taught in the spring of 2003.

The Introduction and Chapter 1 appeared in an earlier form in the article, "Christ Crucified: Lutheran Missiological Themes for a Post-Christian Century," *Currents in Theology and Mission*, April 2003, Vol. 30, #2, pp. 105-118, and in *Mission Studies*, IAMS, Vol. XX—2, 40, 2003, pp. 94-117.

Chapter 4 appeared in a less developed form as "Confessing Jesus Christ within the World of Religious Pluralism," *Bulletin of Missionary Research*, July 1990, p. 115-118.

Chapter 5 was published as a chapter on "Service" in *Mission at the Dawn of the 21st Century*, edited by Paul Varo Martinson, entitled "In the Spirit of Jesus: A Vision Paper on Service and Mission," Kirk House Publishers, 1999, pp.255-267.

The two sermons found in chapter 6 were first preached with a gathering of the Evangelical Lutheran Church in America (ELCA) bishops at St. Mary of the Lake University, Mundelein, Illinois., in January 2003.

Finally, I thank Mary Lou and our entire family for the life-giving experience of love and grace that touches, surrounds, invigorates and inspires me each day of our shared lives.

*Mark Thomsen*
*Shorewood, Wiscconsin*
*January 2004*

# Foreword

In his classic volume, *The Crucified God*, Jürgen Moltmann aptly remarked that the "theologia crucis" is not a single chapter or theme in theology, "but the key-signature of all theology." Such an assertion is obvious to those who are grounded in the theology of the Reformation. But in reality, the theology of the cross has been a neglected theme in Christian theology. Ever since Luther, who in his Heidelberg Disputation came up with the nomenclature "theology of the cross," the theme has been associated with the doctrine of God or the doctrine of atonement. Unfortunately, it has often been interpreted by Luther and others in an individualistic and personal way that the sufferings of Christ are presented as a model and source of meaning for individual trials. In a world that is afflicted by brokenness, violence, pain and suffering, a theology of the cross that is focused solely on individual human sin and guilt tends to trivialize the reality of genuine suffering on the part of millions of men and women. For this reason, the theology of the cross has not been a much-loved topic in Christian theology.

But in recent times there have been many attempts to rehabilitate the centrality of the theology of the cross in theology. Besides Moltmann, theologians like, Kazoh Kitamori, C. S. Song, Kosuke Koyama, Dorothee Sölle, and Douglas John Hall have sought to articulate their theology in relation to Luther's theology of the cross.  At the heart of these recent theological expositions is the view that the theology of the cross is fundamentally about God's abiding commitment to the whole of creation.  These theologies take as their point of departure the brokenness of the human spirit, human community and the created order and place their hope in God's transformative solidarity with life, pain and suffering in the world in order to redeem and make it whole.  These contemporary expositions have thus broadened the focus of the theology of the cross far beyond the concerns of individual salvation so as to include a cosmic thrust to the Christian understanding of the cross. The social, political and global dimensions of the theology of the cross have received greater attention in such expositions.

The present volume, by Mark Thomsen, represents yet another passionate and compassionate articulation of a contemporary theology of the cross, but with a specific focus on the missiology of the cross.  What Thomsen has to say—and says with refreshing clarity—comes out of his background of long pastoral experience, missionary experience, ecumenical involvement, global engagement, and unwavering commitment to the gospel of Jesus Christ.  The volume attempts to articulate a missiology of the cross in relation to Scriptures and the fundamental themes of the Lutheran tradition.   In the process, Thomsen attempts to dialogue with certain insular and rationalistic interpretations of the theology of the cross found among North American Lutherans or representatives of Lutheran Orthodoxy. By stretching the meaning of inherited theological categories in dialogue with contemporary realities, the volume offers a reinterpretation of the theology of the cross relevant for the 21st century.

A contextually relevant missiology of the cross, as Thomsen has argued, must articulate the meaning and challenge of Christian proclamation by taking into account the world of religious pluralism and the tragic identification of the cross with Western Christendom and imperialism.  It must engage in a dialogical witness of both listening and sharing in the midst of people of other faiths.  A missiology of the cross must include the conversation of women and the whole of the global Christian family.  It must seek to witness and serve within a world marked by the horrendous gap between the haves and the have-nothings, the powerful and the vulnerable and must stand in solidarity with the pain and suffering of the world.

Thomsen's missiology of the cross is grounded in a vision of the vulnerable, suffering, saving, transforming God which is able to address and transform life in conformity to the crucified and risen Christ. "This vision through the Spirit," says Thomsen, "has power to transform contemporary humanity marked by alienation, brokenness, enmity and the madness of violence and death. It is this vision that challenges all forms of religious, theological and Christian 'imperialism.' This vision witnesses to Jesus Crucified who came not to be served but to serve and give his life as a ransom (a means of freedom) for many (Mark 10:45)." Those who share this vision, and others too, will find this volume stimulating and insightful.

*J. Paul Rajashekar*
*Lutheran Theological Seminary at Philadelphia*

# Christ Crucified:
## 16th-Century Roots
## for a 21st-Century Missiology of the Cross

The cross is a universal symbol for Christianity as it has encircled the globe. The cross stands on steeples and adorns centers of worship; the cross is found in millions of homes in Japan, China, India, Ethiopia, Nigeria, Uganda, Brazil, Peru, the Island of Fiji, Palestine, Egypt and Iraq as well as in the nations of Europe and North America. Traditional Christianity has interpreted Jesus' death on the cross to have universal saving significance as a means of "atonement" for sin. In some mysterious way Jesus' dying has saving power for the human race.

The cross as a universal symbol, however, does not have universal meaning. Muslims often see the cross as a symbol of a crusading Western power. They view with suspicion Christianity's view of vicarious atonement. They say that God in absolute freedom forgives and is in no need of an atoning sacrifice. The Jewish community sees the cross as a horrifying symbol of Christian persecution and pogroms. It symbolizes their condemnation by many Christians down through history. The charge "Christ-killers" sends shudders down Jewish spines. Asian Hindus, Buddhists and Confucians remember the cross as a symbol of colonialist power emblazoned on flags of the navy of the British Empire. An old British sign in a Shanghai harbor park, "No Dogs or Chinese

Allowed," commemorates that imperial cross. On the other hand, a multitude of Christians inhabiting the poor regions of the third world have seen the cross as a hope-filled symbol of Christ's solidarity with their pain and oppression.

Within such a context of violence, suffering and pluralism, this volume seeks to understand the cross of Jesus as the primary symbol of the mission of God. It accepts the critique that Western Christendom has often been identified with destructive, cultural and colonial domination. However, it argues that an authentic theology of the cross will mold the *Missio Dei*, the mission of God, into the form of "suffering servanthood." The *Missio Dei* is to be cruciformed. It will be aware of the horrendous physical suffering that marks much of the human race, and it will accept God's mission identified in Christ to be in solidarity with the "crucified peoples"[1] and to be committed to eliminate all brokenness, pain and crosses from the world.[2] It will listen for God's truth within every culture and religion. An authentic theology of the cross trusts that God's "crucified Truth"—incarnate and concretized in Jesus—flows from the heart of the universe and is universally present. God can be trusted to be none other than the life-affirming, all-embracing, all-forgiving, vulnerable love heard, seen and touched in the crucified one (I John 1:1-2).

The cross proclaims the crucified Christ as the executed transforming agent of God. It is a paradoxical message asserting that God, the creator of a billion galaxies, is to be encountered in the flesh and blood of a Palestinian Jewish prophet sentenced to death by the political empire of Rome and a small religious hierarchy located in first-century Judea.

This paradoxical proclamation of a crucified personal representative of God (Prophet, Messiah, Christ, Son of God, Servant of God) was created by a miraculous transformation within the early Jesus movement. Jesus' disciples, who had become convinced that he was a special representative of God, came to believe that the one who had been executed in the darkness and wind of a Friday afternoon during Passover festival was not dead but alive! Those who previously had hope, hoped again! (Luke 24:13-35, particularly verse 21). In their resurrection hope the disciples were forced to think of the cross, Jesus' death, as a primary reality within their faith in God. How did the cross of Golgotha, upon which the Lord Jesus hung, fit within the purpose or mission of God? Was

Jesus' cry of abandonment echoed in the broken cry from the God of Galaxies?

The Apostle Paul, one of the earliest writers within the New Testament, determined to preach Christ crucified. Paul writes, "For Jews demand signs and Greeks desire wisdom, but we proclaim Christ crucified, a stumbling block to Jews and foolishness to Gentiles, but to those who are called, both Jews and Greeks, Christ the power of God and the Wisdom of God" (I Cor. 1:22-24).

Paul portrays the power of the cross with multiple images. Paul preaches that "God reconciles us to himself through Christ" (II Cor. 5:18); "but God proves his love for us in that while we were still sinners Christ died for us" (Rom. 5:8); "they are now justified by his grace as a gift, through the redemption which is in Christ Jesus, whom God put forward as an atonement by his blood effective through faith" (Rom. 3:24-25). The followers of Christ are baptized into this costly grace. "Do you not know that all of us who have been baptized into Christ Jesus were baptized into his death? Therefore we have been buried with him by baptism into death, so that, just as Christ was raised from the dead by the glory of the Father, so we too might walk in newness of life" (Rom. 6:3-4).

Within the theological journey of the Christian movement, Martin Luther (1483–1546) was grasped powerfully by Paul's articulation of the gospel centered in the crucified Jesus. For Luther, God's salvation was a gift made possible by the costly sacrifice of the crucified Christ. In response to that costly gift the person of faith was called to die to sin with the crucified and by the power of the Spirit be raised with Jesus into a newness of life in which the fruits of the Spirit are love, faith and hope (I Cor. 13).

This volume is generated by a conversation concerning the theology of the cross within the Christian and in particular the Lutheran tradition. These brief essays are rooted in 16th-century Lutheran theology and express an appreciation for that tradition. However, they challenge the traditional Lutheran perspective to allow Lutheran theological categories to be stretched in new ways as it dialogues with the ecumenical and interfaith context of the 21st century. Lutheran theological language, as in other theological traditions, is loaded with gospel content and may be rearticulated for new times and contexts. The presupposition of these essays is that not only *may* traditional categories be stretched, but they *must* be reformatted so that the crucified Christ as God-with-Us might be more fully known within our post-Constantinian Christian and pluralistic century. It will be argued that this reconstruction is more faithful to the full biblical tradition.

The Lutheran theological tradition, as other Christian traditions, has unique insights to contribute to an understanding of the mission of God. Lutheran missiological themes are rooted in biblical theology; however, they have been molded in powerful and particular ways by the 16th-century context. That context produced creative theological initiatives as well as limitations for attempting to translate a biblical vision of mission into a 21st-century context, a context in which Jesus as the "crucified Truth" is questioned as the future of the human family.

The original 16th-century context included: a medieval piety that claimed that salvation or justification was the consequence of God's action and a required human response of humility or obedience; a medieval church that claimed absolute authority in the areas of both the spiritual and the secular; a church centered in the Roman papacy, which had a vision of the universal or global mission of God and claimed to speak and act on behalf of that mission; and a Protestant Reformation, which included communities whose responses were even more radical than the Lutheran response. Surprisingly, we find that a theology of the cross rooted in this medieval context has the potential for constructing a dynamic foundation for a contemporary vision of the *Missio Dei*.

In order to appreciate and understand the depths of Luther's theology of the cross it is helpful to see the proclamation of the crucified Jesus within the context of four other Lutheran theological emphases.

### Salvation is Sheer Gift: Justification by Grace through Faith

Paul's proclamation of the saving power of the crucified Christ received by faith (I Cor. 1:17, 23-25, Rom. 1:16) became the heart of Luther's theology.[3] Luther rejected the medieval piety that insisted on both a required human act of merit (good works in obedience to the Law) in the process of salvation and an ecclesiastical claim that the church had power through papal indulgences to control humanity's eternal destiny. (It must be clearly stated that much of contemporary Catholic theology has rejected this medieval understanding of the church and salvation.) Lutheran theology is formed by a rejection of these claims; in contrast, it affirms that salvation is totally gift—justification, or being made righteous, is not by works but by grace through faith. This theology directly implies that God loves the world and all sinners; that human life has value, meaning and purpose; and that human relationships with God are not the consequences of human effort but are sheer gift. When grace is received in faith, justification and the transformation of life become realities. Destructive, egocentric life is transformed and becomes Christocentric identification with the mission of God. The focus upon God's grace and salvation as gift is at the heart of the New Testament message. The Jesus movement proclaims that in every time and in every place this gospel has the power to transform life. A Lutheran missiology begins and ends with grace and faith. In a post-Constantinian Christian and pluralistic century it will further explore the depths and breadth of grace in order that the Jesus movement itself might be transformed by the awesome wonder of the gospel!

## The Church Is a Gospel-Created and Gospel-Proclaiming Community

Lutheran theology is molded by its radical critique of the medieval Roman Church embodied in a priestly hierarchy which claimed that the church through the sacraments, validated by the priesthood, enabled all of Christendom to participate in eternal salvation. Furthermore, the Roman Church had a vision of the universal mission of God for which the pope was ultimately responsible. This global mission was to be carried out though the office of bishops, mendicant orders and political institutions, which could be designated by the pope as instruments within the mission of God.

Luther and Lutheran theology rejected this Roman claim as arrogant and demonic. Luther argued that the church was not a transnational, ordained priestly hierarchy but a congregation—community of saints or people of faith—in which Christ is alive and active through the preaching of Good News and the administration of the sacraments. The community designated as church is a gospel-created, gospel-proclaiming people.[4] The whole community is a priesthood responsible for declaring the wonderful acts of God (I Pet. 2:9). The entire community is responsible for the mission outreach of the church. (The "people of God" theme was recaptured by the Catholic Church in the work of Vatican II.) A remarkable illustration of Luther's understanding of mission is seen in his vision of Christian witness among Muslims or Turks. He views this as a lay ministry of evangelism as Christians and Turks intermingle within the conflicts of war. Christians caught behind enemy lines or imprisoned by the Muslims had the opportunity of witnessing to Christ in deeds and also words.[5]

In their reaction to what they saw as papal arrogance, Luther and early Lutherans said that since the time of the apostles no one person had a mandate for carrying out the universal mission of God. Instead, each bishop and pastor had responsibility for the gospel in his own region.[6] The gospel would gradually encircle the world as Christians witnessed through very ordinary means to those with whom they came in contact. For Luther, the gospel did not leapfrog around the world but moved out like waves from the center of a circle created by a stone disturbing the water.[7]

Although Luther's image of mission as waves moving out from a center did not necessarily promote visions of mission beyond the confines of Europe, the analogy has powerful implications for mission within our own communities and societies. With Luther, mission outreach focuses upon lay persons as they engage the world of home, work and society in the name of Jesus. The church is made up of the priesthood of all believers, and as such lay persons are over 99 percent of that priesthood and spend over 98 percent of their time out-side the gathered community. *It is this often unrecognized and scattered community, in their homes and at work in their communities and society, that is on the cutting edge of the mission of the church.* Our congregations, as a gathered priesthood, meet for the purpose of being equipped for mission in the world. As the priesthood gathers, people are healed, equipped, and empowered for their own ministry, which moves into society like leaven in a loaf. Only secondarily is the corporate and institutional community equipped to participate in that mission as an institution or agency.

In the 21st century the laity will not be passionately involved in the institutional mission of the church until the institutional church is passionately concerned about the calling or vocation in daily life of homemakers, students, teachers, farmers, truck drivers, police officers, factory workers, corporate executives, soldiers, lawyers, bankers, builders and nurses. I served as an ELCA staff person for the first eight years of that institution's life. I consider the greatest mistake of those years to be the almost total neglect in developing an adequate program for affirming and equipping lay persons for their mission in the world. The future will focus upon the role of the lay person in the world, or the church will wither in a death spiral of institutional maintenance. If the future belongs to the priesthood of all believers, the clergy and the gathered community will have their opportunity to find their own unique role in the mission of God.[8]

## Creation Is Good and Is the Arena of God's Presence and Mission

The Lutheran affirmation of the God-given value of creation and God's creative law of life embedded in all creation and humanity has given the Lutheran tradition an appreciation for that which is good, beautiful and true in every people, culture and religious tradition. For example, Luther insisted that the natural law summarized in the Ten Commandments was written not only in scripture but in the hearts of all humanity.[9] The natural law called all people to their roles and responsibilities. Marks of God's inner law are manifest in the dignity of life present among Muslims, Jews and others outside the communion centered in Christ, said Luther.

Luther's assertion of the value of creation also came to expression in his insistence that the finite, or creation, has the capacity of holding/embodying the infinite, or God—*finitum capax infiniti*. This insight, emerging from the Protestant debate between Luther and Ulrich Zwingli on the Lord's Supper, reveals the very heart of the biblical faith.[10] God is not only transcendent creator but is present and active "in, with, and under" creation. Creation has God-given value, but it is also the realm of the Holy. Salvation is not to be sought outside the realm of everyday; it is present and engaged within the common and ordinary.

Human activity that has eternal consequences includes feeding the hungry, giving life-giving water to the thirsty, clothing the naked and visiting the lonely (Matt. 25:35ff.). In responding to "the least," one encounters in, with, and under creation the Holy Representative of God who ultimately judges the nations. Visions, miracles and powers are possible, but compassionate involvement in the "suffering least" within the flesh and blood of physical existence is the essential dimension of the mission of God.

Luther captured the centrality of the common and secular when he said that all baptized Christians belong to one priesthood and are only distinguished by the role or occupation that they have within the community. A shoemaker, a smith, and a farmer have a God-given calling within their occupations as well as the priest or bishop.[11] Here and now one is justified, and here and now one is grasped by the infinite and swept into creation and humanity in order to participate in the new creation (II Cor. 5:16-20). Here in flesh and blood, stuff and matter, one meets the gracious and calling God and participates in the mission of God by following God's servant, Jesus. It is this biblical, creation-centered perspective that calls the Jesus movement into mission. Luther himself practiced and celebrated that divine secularity as he led monks and nuns out of convents and monasteries into challenging vocations in the world.

### Hold to Christ and for the Rest Be Totally Uncommitted

Lutheran tradition has not bound the gospel to particular rites, ceremonies or institutional forms. According to the Augsburg Confession, Article VII, it is sufficient for the unity of the church to agree on the preaching of the gospel and the administration of the sacraments. Cultural forms that have molded rites, ceremonies, theological symbols and ecclesiastical structures are *adiaphora*, nonessential, and may change as the gospel moves from one context to another. In the words of Herbert Butterfield (who is not a Lutheran), "Hold to Christ and for the rest be totally uncommitted."[12] This evangelical freedom enables a Lutheran missiology to enter every new context with freedom and flexibility in order to proclaim and live the gospel in ways that are relevant and meaningful to the new community of faith.

Lutherans have not always taken advantage of this freedom but again and again have allowed themselves to be imprisoned in the cultural and theological forms of the 16th and 17th centuries. The Augsburg Confession had said that the gospel was to be preached in its purity and the sacraments rightly administered. Orthodoxy identified "purity" and "rightly" with 16th- and 17th-century cultural forms. The adherents of Lutheran orthodoxy often became so focused upon "purity" and "rightly" as they were imprisoned in the past that they lost sight of the mission of God which had been birthed in a Semitic culture and which, within a generation, thought and spoke theology in Greek. It is essential to recognize that *only a church with the capacity for cultural change and adaptability has the potential for being a faithful instrument of the Missio Dei. It is only when a theological tradition forms a foundation rather than a fortress that it can speak to a post-Christian and pluralistic century.*

### Luther's 16th-Century Theology of the Cross.

In his radical critique of the Roman Church Luther developed a theology of the cross, or, in his own words, he described being a theologian of the cross.[13] The most explicit presentation of this perspective is found in the Heidelberg Disputation, where Luther emphasized:

- the God of the gospel appears in weakness as the crucified Jesus;
- in this crucified Jesus, the sinner is grasped by grace and is justified apart from the law or human attempts to justify the self;
- revelation of the true God is in the crucified Jesus and not in reason, which claims to find God in the splendor of creation and the natural order;
- good works do not lead to salvation; rather, Christians must exercise extreme care to avoid being deceived into self-justification by good works;
- as Jesus lived in weakness and was subjected to suffering, the Christian should expect the same in life; and suffering is God's way of driving humans to the foot of the cross;
- Christ who lives in persons through faith creates good works within and though them.

In his theology of the cross Luther emphasized that salvation was God's gift through Jesus, the Christ, whose suffering and death made justification and the conquest of death a reality. God's saving power was revealed in seeming weakness as the Son of God hung on a cross. Luther spoke of seeing the back side of God since the crucified Son did not appear to manifest the power of God. This focus upon the hiddenness of God and the suffering of the Son has tremendous value in articulating a missiology for the 21st century. It speaks to a world that experiences lostness, suffering, oppression, and the seeming absence of God. However, a 21st-century theology of the cross is relevant to the world of the West and particularly the U.S.A., which avoids—like the plague—and denies—as much as possible—the presence of suffering and evil in life. Too often within the Western church the cross of the crucified and the crucified people is hidden behind dollar signs and happy faces.

Luther's own theology is grounded in his own intense personal religious experience. It concentrates upon the individual sinner in the presence of God. Luther's theology of the cross, which has been so powerful in making possible the transformation of the individual sinner's life, focused on the sinner's absolute need for the gift of justification and the sinner's capacity in self-deception to use good works in attempting to justify the self. In developing his thought Luther used the Pauline image of dying to an old self in order that the sinner might be raised as a transformed, new, living self of faith (Rom. 6:1ff.).

Luther's thought, rooted in a 16th-century medieval piety which has contributed richly to the evangelical message, is so centered upon the self that it fails to see the theology of the cross as a missiological resource beyond preaching justification by faith. The preaching of justification is a powerful dimension of the theology of the cross; however, it is a much richer resource for mission than that which is articulated by Luther. Chapter 1 suggests theological resources and ways in which a contemporary missiology may tap a broader understanding of a theology of the cross and its significance for the mission of God.[14]

## CHAPTER 1

# The Pain of the World,

## the Suffering of God and the Cross of Jesus

### Jesus Crucified for a 21st- Century Missiology

A biblical understanding of the cross and the mission of the church is a powerful way in which to attempt to develop a biblical missiology for our time and context. Jon Sobrino, the Catholic Latin American liberation theologian, has done precisely that in articulating a mission theology molded by the cross for his context. Sobrino develops themes such as the suffering and death of God, God's solidarity with the oppressed, God's conflict with evil, and the vulnerability of the Servant and servants of God.[15] Interestingly, he writes that he has been accused of being influenced by the Lutheran tradition. He replies that a theology of the cross is central to the biblical message.

In developing a theology of the cross for the 21st-century mission context, a number of significant factors within the contemporary situation must be addressed.

- *Religious pluralism is a global reality* with two-thirds of six billion people being in a variety of religious communities. This pluralism raises the question as to the validity of religious experience, revelation and salvation within and outside a particular "household of faith." Alternative answers need to be explored in order to make possible an authentic witness to the gospel.
- *Religious pluralism is a challenge to our understanding of the Missio Dei.* Within this world of pluralism, the cross has

been a symbol of Christianity. Tragically, it has been seen as a symbol of Western and "Christian" military, political and economic power. The fact that the flag of the British Empire was marked by a cross reinforced this identification of faith with politics. A missiology of the cross will deconstruct this demonic imperialism of Western Christendom.

- *There is a horrendous global divide* between the powerful who possess and the weak who have been dispossessed. This widening gap must be challenged by any Jesus movement, particularly because some Lutheran missiologies have understood justice issues as peripheral to the heart of the gospel.

- *There is a dying Christendom* identified with Western secularism in contrast to a global church that encircles the world and is alive, speaking and acting in a thousand new cultural contexts and forms. The demographic center of the church has actually shifted from the northern hemisphere to the southern. Over 60 percent of the Christian community now live in Africa, Asia and Latin America. The dying Christendom of the West will ignore this spiritual awakening at the risk of its own survival.

- *Evil, divisive powers manifest* in violent conflicts, racism and sexism permeate all of life. Participants in the Reign of God will identify all evil structures and powers destructive of life in order to challenge them in the name of Christ.

- *The changing role and status of women* force the church and society to hear new voices and rethink old values and theologies in order that all human resources might be enlisted in the mission of God.

- *The world of materialism* is a spiritual desert, and the Western church is often more fully integrated into that relativistic, materialistic, militaristic desert than into the life-giving kingdom of God.

- A *postmodern world dominated by the scientific exploration* of the cosmos has infinitely expanded our vision of reality and God; however, it often has abandoned speaking of a Reality that is the sacred source or ground of all of life.

A theology of the cross within a post-Constantinian Christian 21st century has the possibility of pointing to an awesome Mystery that transcends our local deities. If this

Mystery cannot be accepted, it will at least be longed for by every human heart. Only a seemingly hidden, suffering-servant God is a realistic vision for a world marked by pain and absurdity. It is within this contemporary context that this missiology of the cross is explored.

## A Theology of the Cross for the 21st Century— What it Is Not!

A theology of the cross should not glorify suffering and death, although Christian theology has often done just that. Recently, several feminist theologians have severely critiqued horrendous and distorted understandings of the cross, which they describe as divine child abuse.[16] They reference atonement theories in which the Father punishes the innocent Son in order that God's honor might be restored or retributive justice might be fulfilled. Some feminist theologians argue that an abusive heavenly Father legitimizes abusive earthly fathers. There is no question that this type of theology is prevalent within Christianity and has led to destructive consequences for abused persons and to the legitimization of retaliation within social and political relationships. In contrast to this "Anselmian" theology, an authentic theology of the cross affirms that life and the transformation of life, not suffering and death, are the ultimate purposes of God. An authentic theology of the cross is a celebration of the value of life, life that is worth living and even dying for.

The reign of God is embodied in Jesus as Jesus through the Spirit challenges powers that are destructive of life. He heals the sick, cleanses lepers, makes the blind see and the crippled walk, center-stages the marginalized, empowers the weak, forgives the ostracized and 'damned,' and creates a reconciled community. In the words of John 10:10, "I have come that they might have life, and have it abundantly." This transformation of life through the Spirit's power is the purpose of God. Within this mission context theology will reaffirm a positive theology of creation. The theology of the cross is to be placed within God's creative and sustaining work; within humanity's potential, which is rooted in the "image of God;" within the kingdom of God, which transforms a broken humanity; and within the story of our cosmos with the possibility of billions of Big-Bang universes.

Second, a theology of the cross is not the reiteration of an Anselmian doctrine of the atonement. The suffering of the Son is not to be interpreted as the propitiation of the wrath of God that now makes possible what was impossible, the forgiveness of sin, although Luther certainly accepts this view.[17] An authentic theology of the cross is rooted in the biblical tradition that God's saving transformation of broken life flows from God's passionate love for sinful humanity and the world. Love, not wrath, is the primary reality we identify with God. Love as passionate care for life is the origin and redemption of life. "For God so loved the world that God gave his only Son…" (John 3:16); "But God shows his love for us in that while we were yet sinners Christ died for us" (Rom. 5:8); "God was in Christ reconciling the world [to Godself]" (II Cor. 5:18); "In this is love not that we loved God but God loved us and sent God's son to be an expiation for our sin" (I John 4:10, 22). However one thinks of atonement, it must be seen as originating in the eternal compassion and love of God.

How then does one respond to questions concerning the anger or the wrath of God? God's wrath as the anger of God against evil and sin is an expression of love that intends to recreate life and transform a fractured and tortured world. Love expressed as wrath for whatever tortures life manifests God's passionate concern for, rather than indifference and distance from, the pain of life. Love that seeks solidarity with suffering people and contests that which destroys life is the cosmic wellspring from which salvation flows.[18]

Third, Luther believes that suffering is an expression of God's wrath for the purpose of driving people to the foot of the cross. This view cannot be universalized because of the ambiguities and complexities of experience. Although suffering may shake people's confidence in themselves and may move them to God, and although destructive actions may lead to self-destruction, suffering and death cannot always be identified with the judgment of God. A contemporary theology of the cross must also speak more clearly of the consequences of evil or the demonic as they are embodied within the protagonists and peoples of history.[19]

Fourth, the theology of the cross is not simply a doctrine of the atonement. It is much more than that. It redefines God, the Christ, the *Missio Dei*, the church, everything. The cross is the primary key for interpreting the whole of Christian thought and praxis.

Finally, the theology of the cross is rooted not only in particular biblical passages concerning the saving effects of Jesus' death but in Jesus' total life, mission, death, and resurrection understood within the prophetic faith of Israel. The missiology of the cross is embedded within the story of God's mission embodied in Jesus.

## A Theology of the Cross for the 21st Century— What it Might Be!

The cross means dying to private dreams in order to participate in the vision of the kingdom of God. A theology of the cross is grounded in the prayer of Jesus that led to his cross: "Not my will but your will be done." The Gospels witness to the reality that Jesus' mission and death were not the private dream of a Jewish carpenter but were rooted in the vision of the Reality whom Jesus addressed as "Father." If nothing else, Jesus was a person possessed by the reality of God. Jesus believed that he was called by God, empowered by the Spirit of God, led by God, even if it meant being faithful to a vision that ultimately led to the horror of Golgotha. Jesus witnessed to God, spoke of God; the central theme of his proclamation was the kingdom of God; and his most powerful gift was a baptism into the Spirit of God. From the perspective of Jesus and the early disciples, Jesus surrendered his heart, mind, will and life to God. The cross signified dying to personal dreams and visions in order to be open to the reign of God.

Paul would use this theme of dying to the old and being raised to the new creation as a way of communicating the gospel within the mystery religions of the Roman Empire. Luther used that Pauline theme to focus on the theme of "personally dying and rising with Christ." Luther's theology of the cross focuses upon this personal dimension and does not explore the wider missionary significance of the cross. A theology of the cross for the 21st century will use the theme of dying and rising to speak of dying to personal, corporate, ethnic, and nationalistic egocentric dreams in order to participate in the *Missio Dei*, in God's vision of a new creation. Christian discipleship is dying to an old self or reality with limited, distorted and destructive dreams in order to be conformed to the cruciformed mission of the kingdom of God.

*A theology of the cross announces that God is in solidarity with life, pain and suffering in the world.* The resurrection confirms that the way and word of Jesus, which culminates in his crucifixion, is God's way of being present and active in the world. God's identity is defined not out of a philosophical tradition but in Jesus' living and Jesus' dying. The resurrection faith trusts that Jesus is fully transparent to the present and living God. God's identifying with Jesus' dying means that God has entered into total solidarity with the human family, even into the depths of human pain, suffering and death. The biblical faith does not limit this compassion ("agonizing-with") to a few moments of suffering on the cross but traces the depths of this solidarity from antiquity to the present. God heard the cries of ancient Israel and knew (experienced) its suffering (Exod. 3:7-8). God weeps over the desolation of Israel where people, cattle and birds no longer are seen or heard (Jer. 9:10). God passionately cared for the population and cattle of Nineveh, graciously desiring their salvation (Jonah). God's compassion sweeps through history as the *Missio Dei*. It was embodied in Jesus' mission, vividly expressed as Jesus wept over Jerusalem (Luke 19:41), and is present wherever suffering and pain are present in life today (Matt. 25:31ff.).[20] Suffering often marks that which is destructive of life. However, "suffering-with" marks love that is so deep that it is moved by the pain of the other and enters into the suffering of the other for the transformation of life.

Jesus' own suffering and cross participated in the pain-love of God (a phrase used by Asian theologian C. S. Song) that is the Ultimate Reality within a broken, pain-filled cosmic order.[21] This emphasis on the suffering of God and the cross of Jesus must be viewed within a theology in which God values life and creation. As noted above, Lutheran theology recognizes the world of flesh and blood as the location of the sacred where salvation as a new creation is birthed. It is significant that multitudes of people living under conditions of oppression have intuitively been grasped by this dimension of Jesus crucified. Black slaves sang of the one who knew their suffering:

> They nail my Jesus down,
> They put him on the Cross of Thorns.
> O see my Jesus hangin' high!
> He look so pale an' bleed so free;
> O don't you think it was a shame,
> He hung three hours in dreadful pain?[22]

Similarly, the outcasts within Indian society see God suffering in solidarity with the "crushed ones," or Dalits, of India.[23] Women around the globe celebrate the God who identifies with the oppressed and dispossessed of the world.[24]

God's solidarity with brokenness springs out of God's passionate concern for the world. A church marked by and enticed by a comfortable life and mountaintop experiences apart from pain-filled valleys, is irrelevant to the *Missio Dei.* An authentic Christianity, in the words of Dietrich Bonhoeffer, is called to share the suffering of God in the world![25]

**The cross means that sin as embodied evil has immense power in the world.** Identifying the mission and death of Jesus with the reign of God means that faith experiences and acknowledges that sin as embodied evil has incredible power in the world. God's very best is pushed out of life and onto a cross. Past and contemporary history manifests this continuing power of evil, embodied in the historical antagonists to life, as the good, the true and the beautiful are crushed again and again. People of the cross will seek to identify and acknowledge the presence of the creative word of God within all creation and all human cultures and religions. They will also fearlessly name evil in all of its forms, personal sin (beginning with ourselves) and structural sin (the idols of the nations). As sinful, yet forgiven, participants in the reign of God they will struggle against the forces of Satan in every context in order that life might be transformed. A contemporary theology of the cross will reclaim Luther's own acceptance of demonic reality and humanity's struggle with evil.

Gustaf Aulén's classic theory of the atonement recognizes this divine-demonic clash, but fails to place that clash in the midst of history and life.[26] The clash, however, can never be simply identified with ethnic, political, national or international clashes within history. It is a conflict far deeper—between the Abba and Spirit of Jesus and demonic powers that are destructive of God's gift of love and life.

**God is in a prophetic, messianic struggle against evil.** The resurrection identifies the mission and death of Jesus with the prophetic-messianic reign of God, and the Spirit manifests that God is in a life-and-death struggle with evil. "But if it is by the Spirit of God that I cast out demons, then the kingdom of God has come to you" (Matt. 12:27; cf. Luke 11:20). Jesus is crucified as a direct consequence of his prophetic ministry, his messianic mission against the powers of darkness. Jesus challenged those religious and political values and institutions of his era that limited, impoverished or destroyed life. Jesus combated legalistic religious authorities who relegated sinners and the spiritually marginalized to the realm of eternal destruction and the sick and unclean to societal oblivion. Jesus engaged and challenged the rich and powerful who dominated and manipulated the weak and dispossessed. Jesus challenged the cultic priesthood that secularized and commercialized an ancient faith tradition intended to bring humanity into communion with God. Jesus frightened imperial Roman representatives who saw him as a source of unrest and rebellion within an unstable province of the East. Jesus' prophetic mission enraged his opponents, and they conspired to destroy him (Mark 3:6). They crushed Jesus by hanging him on a cross.

*Jesus was not sent to die; he came to live and challenge Satan and all his powers.* Jesus was crucified in God's struggle for righteousness, truth and the transformation of life. The resurrection is the sign of hope in the midst of a raging battle that God ultimately will have God's will done. Therefore, we hopefully pray, "Your kingdom come; your will be done!" That prayer leads to conformity with the cruciform mission of God. It leads in every new context to an involvement in the mission of God's struggle for justice, righteousness and the transformation of life.

The Lutheran theological tradition has usually emphasized that Jesus came to die rather than that he was sent to fulfill a mission that culminated in his death. In interpreting Jesus in this way, Christianity was seen as that faith which offered a means of facing death without the fear of the judgment of God. Lutherans more often than not prepared for death and the afterlife. A missiology for the 21st century will prepare the church for its struggle against the life-destroying demonic in this world with the incredible promise that if you lose your life in it you will share the death-transcending victory of the reign of God! (Mark 8:35)

**God wills to be vulnerable in the world.** A theology of the cross asserts that in this struggle against evil, God limits Godself to the power of noncoercive, persevering love in bringing forth the new creation. Out of the depths of compassion Jesus cared, spoke, preached, touched, healed, exorcised, raged, and turned over tables. But he did not attempt to lead a violent revolution in order to establish a political kingdom in the midst of the Roman Empire. Rather, Jesus' reign-of-God revolution included the power to name evil, confront powers, heal and empower people, love and weep over enemies even as he was nailed to the cross.

This reign of God is solidly and passionately in the world but is not of the world. Within this present age the Messiah and the Messiah's followers do not seek to coercively impose the will of God upon the earth. One Chinese communist party member said to me, "You cannot possibly run a country this way." That is absolutely correct. You cannot run a political institution without the use of coercive power. Jesus recognized that his kingdom is not of this world; it belongs to a different order of being. Instead of building a new world through law and order, God through the Spirit creates a servant-people who permeate the world and undermine the values and institutions that destroy life in order that a new creation might appear. It is this cruciform *Missio Dei,* embodied in Jesus, that can be identified with Jesus' vision of the coming reign of God. The reign of God will not be politically institutionalized in a Zionism or Christendom, but, like salt, leaven and light, will be loose in the world. This messianic reign will always be vulnerable to the coercive forces of evil. Nevertheless, it will cross cultural, political and ethnic lines. The new creation of authentic community and relationships can never be imposed coercively, but must be drawn out of human beings by the Spirit. The Spirit creates new relationships that embrace even "the enemy."[27]

For three hundred years, the Jesus movement lived out this nonviolent, vulnerable mission of Jesus. Today this faith tradition is courageously lived out in the pacifist Christian communities that continue to follow Jesus by rejecting all forms of political violence.[28] Early Christianity was transformed when Emperor Constantine in 313 made a previously persecuted faith the established religion of the Roman Empire. Suddenly bishops called upon their pacifist communities to take up swords and defend the Empire.[29] How could the followers of Jesus live in this new world? Lutheran theology has had a unique answer to that question.

**Two reigns of God.** God intends to bring forth a totally different order of being: a new age, a new creation, and a new way of relating. However, from a traditional Lutheran perspective this does not exclude God from continuing to preserve "the present age" or "the old creation." In order to keep the present age from self-destructing while a new age is being born, God may use and does use coercive power. People of faith are swept into this life and find themselves called to be participants in the struggle to maintain the present age from self-destruction. They make laws and enforce them in order to preserve community and life. Luther calls this the kingdom/reign of God's left hand. The followers of Jesus also experience being called as participants into God's messianic mission to bring forth a new creation through a vulnerable mission of love. That mission is made concrete in gospel words of love, forgiveness, challenge, and hope and in noncoercive actions of compassion and justice. Luther called this God's reign of the right hand. Commenting on this two-fold reign of God, he said: In participating in the right hand of God's work, I am called in my personal life to turn the other cheek. But when called to participate in the work of the left hand of God I am not called to turn my neighbor's cheek.[30]

For Luther, God is ambidextrous. God is motivated by love in acting with both right and left hands. With God's left hand, God is struggling with coercive force against powers that threatened physical life itself. With God's right hand, God is in Christ bringing a new order of being into reality. The gospel is preached and with acts of love and compassion brings forth a new creation. Thus, Luther addressed the complexity by speaking of the two reigns of God.[31]

For the 21st century, the cruciformed *Missio Dei*, the kingdom of God's right hand, will embody the vulnerability of God incarnate in Jesus. *Particularly in relating to people of other faiths, the body of Christ will denounce every manifestation of imperialistic Christendom ,and with Jesus will be a serving and reconciling community.* In the words of an African proverb, the Jesus movement will walk softly into a distant place. There will continue to be pacifist Christians, like Martin Luther King Jr., who identify with the nonviolent agenda of Jesus in the most violent situations. There will be others who, like Luther, believe they are called to participate in an ambiguous world within two reigns of God. However, the right-handed cruciformed *Missio Dei* will reject every effort to identify the reign of God initiated by Jesus with an ethnic, nationalistic, political or ideological agenda. No one in the name of Christ can implement a nationalistic program because no one can use the name of the Abba of Jesus to speak exclusively for a fraction of the human race. Nor can anyone in the name of the nonviolent Christ fight a war—even against terrorists (Matt. 5:38-48). Wars will always be fought in the name of only a fraction of the human race ("national security") and always involve violence and brutality that crush human lives. Most Christians and Lutherans have sought to justify the horror of war by claiming that love must defend life from an even greater evil.[32] Lutherans have spoken of the necessity of law, order and warfare as the work of God's left-handed rule. However, the ambiguity of "just war," the fusion of good with evil, the difficulty of loving the neighbor while taking their lives or killing their babies in bomb attacks, should make it seem absurd to fight any war in the name of the God incarnate in Jesus the Christ. Most wars are fought for security of a fraction of the human race and only should be fought in the name of that nation's security and peace. Some wars supposedly have been fought to end all wars and achieve global peace. Even within these "justified" wars, prayers during war can only be cries to God for mercy and forgiveness, cries of supplication for life and peace for all.

**Theodicies and the atonement.** A theology of the cross proclaimed by a resurrection faith implies that even though righteousness and compassion are repeatedly crushed within history, the light and love of the reign of God is never snuffed out or eliminated. The vulnerable reign of God is present and hidden even within the darkest tragedies and absurdities and has the potential of reemerging to defy the powers of darkness. The resurrection of Jesus and the present power of the Spirit are God's promise that the reign of God marked by compassion and vulnerability, always comes back and ultimately will prevail. This means that in the world of theodicies (attempts to explain evil) faith trusts that there is light and life within and on the other side of tragedy and death. Faith may not have rationales for defeats, suffering and death; however, faith hopes and within tears rejoices that since Christ lives, we, too, do and will live.[33]

This also means that atonement theologies will always affirm that God will never fail to bear responsibility for the divine-human relationship; God will not let us go! Atonement theology focuses upon the fact that God not only suffers with us, but God suffers because of our sins and for our sins. God's love embraces not only the victims but also the victimizers, not only Rachel's children but also Saul of Tarsus the persecutor of the church. The resurrection is the promise that, even though God's chosen one has been despised and rejected, God has not deserted this sin-filled planet, nor humanity, nor individuals, all having infinite worth. God persistently returns in suffering grace. In love God has chosen to absorb into God's own being all of the hate and rebellion of the human family. Within God's own being God carries and bears the sins of the world. It is this divine bearing of sins, divine responsibility-taking, that makes forgiveness, justification and life possible. John points to Jesus as the incarnation of this reality and says, "Behold, the Lamb of God who takes away the sin of the world" (John 1:29). God whispers from eternity, "You may not wish my blessing, but I will go through hell to give it to you." God will never let us go! This understanding of the atonement asserts that *God* is in Christ reconciling the world to Godself (I Cor. 5:18-21). Any atonement theory in which Christ is not transparent to the Abba of Jesus, but in some way transforms the Father's attitude to humanity, must be seen as a contradiction of the gospel.

A number of recent theologians have articulated a vision of the atonement in similar images. The Japanese theologian Kitamori speaks of God as grieving over God's children. God grieves because even though God's wrath wills to purge us of sin as we destroy one another, God in love refuses to give us up. Grieving love wills to bear our sinful brokenness and will not let us go![34] Douglas John Hall describes God's suffering love embracing humanity who, in freedom, choose to walk contrary to the will of God. God refuses to forfeit the relationship distorted by human sin and instead chooses to bear the sin of humanity.[35] Jürgen Moltmann describes the suffering of the Father who wills to send the Son into the world. The Father "gives up/over" the Son to a suffering mission resulting in death because only a vulnerable mission can reconcile humanity without destroying human freedom and therefore humans themselves. Rather than destroy the human community, the Father and Son, in suffering, bear the sins of the world.[36] In very similar terms, Elizabeth Johnson speaks of God's suffering love as the power to resist evil and continue to create anew.[37] The cross testifies to a love that will not let us go. A pain-love that bears humanity's unwillingness to be conformed to the image of God is sheer grace!

This understanding of the atonement has nothing to do with the glorification of suffering or divine child abuse. It has nothing to do with the appeasement of a God of wrath. It has everything to do with divine compassion, which is so powerful and deep that love spontaneously embraces all humanity, bears the rebelliousness of a broken world, and struggles as leaven within the loaf of creation and humanity to transform the totality of reality.

***The pain-filled cost of vulnerability in a hope-filled mission.*** Feminist theologians have critiqued traditional atonement theories as representing cosmic child abuse. God causes God's Christ or Son to suffer. However, there is another way of interpreting the sending of the Son in a mission marked by suffering. God intends to transform reality from within, through persevering love struggling for compassion, righteousness and justice. Into this transforming mission, God sends vulnerable human instruments of the kingdom of God—Jesus the Christ, the body of Christ and the unrecognized and hidden servants of God. They are the vulnerable power confronting the nonvulnerable resistance of the kingdom of evil embodied in sinful humanity. To send vulnerable servants is like sending sheep into the midst of wolves (Matt. 10:16). However, God, whose love embraces the totality of life, including both sheep and wolves, calls a vulnerable company of "militant" pacifists to enter a struggle where the sheep will be abused, beaten and killed in order that human lives and community might be transformed. The sending Father agonizes with and for the vulnerable company of witnesses and weeps and cries out at their death. The agony of the God of the galaxies resonates to the cries from the cross. It is the divine and human cost of God's mission of reconciliation.[38]

Where then is hope? Hope is rooted in the resurrection promise that God raised Jesus from death. It is also rooted in the gift of the Spirit that transformed frightened followers into dynamic witnesses. An early disciple on the Emmaus road reported to the "unrecognized" Jesus who had accompanied them, "We had hoped that he was the one to redeem Israel" (Luke 24:21). There on the road they no longer hoped. But the resurrection made it possible for them to hope again. "Jesus is risen and has spoken to Simon" (Luke. 24.35). They reported that many had seen him; the twelve had seen him; Mary had seen him; Paul had seen him (I Cor. 15:1-11). Furthermore, the Risen One had poured out the Spirit of God that God had given him. Faith, hope and love were alive (I Cor. 13). Victories over fear and the powers of darkness were a reality. As in Jesus, spiritual power was activated and the gospel was proclaimed, forgiveness announced, the crippled walked, demons were exorcized, the marginalized center-staged, and those who had fled (terrified as Jesus approached the cross) defied death for the sake of the reign of God. Vulnerable witnesses trusted that their struggles, their deaths, their witnesses, their martyrdoms were shared by the pain-love of the God of galaxies. They participated in the sufferings of Christ and continued to complete the suffering mission of Christ (Col. 1:24).

**Expanding the scope of God's grace concretized in the Crucified Truth.** Within this awesome vision one wonders why we as Lutheran Christians have, in our witness to Jesus, so limited the breadth and scope of God's all-embracing love, the crucified Truth. Why did the church, initially sharing a cosmic and universal Christ, then, beginning with Cyprian and for centuries after, continue to announce that outside the church there is no salvation? Why did Luther in his explanation to the Third Article of the Creed in the Large Catechism say "but outside the Church [that is, where the Gospel is not] there is no forgiveness and hence no holiness"? Why would one possibly conceive that the grace that embraced Paul as he murdered Christians would not embrace those who were not even aware that the Abba of the universe was the source of their own lives and hope? Why would one limit the "love that will never let us go" to those who encountered Jesus personally or in an authentic witness to Jesus? Is the grace of God concretized in Jesus not unconditional? Is it after all conditioned by historical contingency, the time and place of one's birth, or one's spiritual response? These questions are particularly significant as the Jesus community moves into the 21st century.

Questions are not raised because one must assume parity within the religions of the world. They also are not raised because one must accept the absolute relativism of a postmodern world. Rather, the questions are raised because of our convictions and hope that the life-transforming power of serving love concretized in Jesus ultimately is the very presence and activity of the Abba and Spirit of the universe. Because faith trusts that Jesus is transparent to the Abba and Spirit of the universe, faith trusts that the Heart of the universe (God) is and never will be other than the love incarnate in Jesus. Faith may trust that for one's own self, and, much more significantly, faith may trust that for the whole universe and every human family and person. All of life is embraced by that same love. Would not all of life then live within that same acceptance and forgiveness? Evangelism is sharing this gift: "May I tell you a mystery of the universe that you may not know but which already has grasped you?" Such a vision explodes our limited theological agenda, for we are certain that in Jesus we have not encountered an ethnic, national, or religious (not even Christian) deity, but the ultimate Mystery and Wisdom of the totality of cosmic reality.

This faith vision is not threatened by the possibility of intelligent life forms scattered throughout trillions of stars and galaxies. Our knowledge of the universe is exploding. Soon we will be talking of a multitude of Big-Bang cosmic constructs and the reality of countless havens of intelligent life. How does one speak of God's life-creating and transforming power one trillion light years away in a galaxy unknown to our time and space? Is creative and transforming love within this mystery to be conditioned upon a human mission endeavor traveling at time-warp speeds, collapsing time and space? If so, a multitude of eternities will lapse before that is a possibility. Limiting salvation to those who encounter the Jesus of the Gospels is placing Jesus in a very tiny theological package addressed to a small fraction of the human family within a small corner of the universe. The Abba of Jesus actually comes in a gigantic "box," inclusive of a multitude of cultures and universes and addressed to a multiplicity of peoples and intelligent life forms. Placing the finality of Jesus within the meta-cosmic Abba of Jesus does not minimize the mystery of the Incarnation, but transposes it into an intercultural and interstellar symphony.

This awesome vision of faith will not limit God's compassionate embrace and power within our global life to those who belong to Christian institutions, or those who make statements about their faith in Jesus. Our world is shrinking into a global village, and those of us in the West or North are increasingly aware of peoples of other faiths and traditions. We experience a variety of gifts among the peoples of other faiths that, according to our biblical tradition, are manifestations of the presence and power of the Abba and Spirit of the universe, identified by the resurrection hope as the Abba and Spirit of Jesus. We also are deeply disturbed by the fact that the message of God's vulnerable love in Christ that has grasped us is not the message that millions of people around the globe have heard us proclaim. The crucified servant Jesus has been hidden and distorted by an imperialistic Christendom and a Western philosophical rationalism. When Christianity becomes identified with U.S. cultural arrogance, political exploitation and militaristic domination, suddenly the crucified Jesus has become the cosmic warrior carrying the stars and stripes with power to raise and destroy earthly kingdoms by overwhelming military power. Our "Christian" proclamation then implies heavenly tyranny rather than the God willing to be vulnerable unto death in order to transform life from within.

Living within the incredible vision of God's grace and this horrifying distortion of Jesus crucified will have powerful consequences for living within the world of religious diversity. For example, one will never be totally surprised by the wonders of life that may appear in Galaxy 70097 or in any of the communities of the world's religions. One expects that the Abba and Spirit of Jesus have already and always been there. Furthermore, as Abraham was blessed by the unknown King of Righteousness, Melchizedek, we may expect to be blessed by people within every religious family. This does not mean that evil and sin are not also universally present and may be encountered any and everywhere in every form of religion, including Christendom. We should not then be surprised to be challenged by insights and truth encountered outside the Christian family. For example, Martin Luther King Jr. found inspiration in the Hindu Ghandi, a prophet of nonviolence who had been "captured" by the Spirit of Jesus. It seems clear that the Abba and Spirit of the universe raised up a prophet in India who, not only transformed a nation by a nonviolent struggle, but understood Jesus, has something to teach the whole Christian community. Who then is closer to the Spirit of Jesus?

An affirmation of the wider scope of God's grace embodied in the crucified and risen Christ will not squelch evangelism. On the contrary, a community possessed with such a vision will persistently and powerfully share this vision. Who would not wish to share this vision of God? If God is this deeply united with all creation—this passionately wrapped up with all of life; willing to go this far into human existence, even to the death of the cross; powerful enough to continually bring new life out of death; gracious enough to call humanity into participation in this cosmic adventure—why would we keep that to ourselves?

Evangelism is proclaiming, sharing and living this vision, this cosmic reality, this God concretized in Jesus Crucified. Evangelism announces, shares and lives in the assurance that the serving, creative, caring, justice-seeking divine love seen, heard and touched in Jesus is universally present. As Augustine writes in his dissertation on the Trinity (Second Book, Chapter 5), "The Son (Logos) came [broke into our human sphere of reality] to where the Son already was." The Logos of the gospel reveals what is everywhere present, everywhere bringing light, everywhere pointing to and witnessing to that which is the true light coming into and enfleshed in the world (John 1:1-14).

This awesome vision of the mystery of God is not new. It is already present in the New Testament and in the early church. The writers of Ephesians and Colossians placed Jesus within this metacosmic reality. The God embodied in Jesus was the God unifying the totality of all reality (Eph. 1, Col. 1). The God incarnate in Jesus is the Abba who is everywhere and always present and active in the world. A quick glimpse at the biblical tradition reveals that this universal theme is a basic dimension of the biblical faith. Within the tradition of the Pentateuch an unknown king, designated Melchizedek, or the King of Righteousness (Gen. 14), blessed Abraham, the father of faith; and Jethro, the Priest of Midian and father-in-law of Moses; taught the people of Israel organizational skills for the new community (Exod. 18). Within the prophets, Amos saw God as the Lord of all nations calling and guiding all the nations of Israel's world (Amos 9:7), and Isaiah saw Cyrus, the king of Persia, as God's servant (Isa. 45:1).

Within the New Testament tradition Jesus, Paul, and the writer of I Peter understood salvation as a dynamic power through which God was universally at work in the world (the whole cosmos). However, God's transforming power, which became incarnate in Christ, was not limited to the historical

Christian movement. Jesus, like the Old Testament writers, saw God's saving presence outside the community of Abraham's descendants or his own ministry. In Luke 4:24-30 it is reported that Jesus sees God's saving work in a widow from Sidon and a Syrian military officer, an observation that nearly cost him his life at the hands of those who had God locked up in a tiny ethnic box. In Luke 10:25-37, Jesus describes a despised Samaritan as the embodiment of God-intended compassion—even for the enemy. In Luke 18:9-14, Jesus declares a sinner to be justified and forgiven even though he may have been totally unaware of that fact. In Matthew 25:31-45, Jesus teaches that multitudes from all nations are pronounced as participants in God's final victory, even though they had not been aware of their encounters with the reign of God. It would appear that if one takes Jesus seriously, faith in the finality of Christ necessarily includes the recognition of God's creative saving work outside of hearing and believing in Jesus Christ.

The traditional understanding of salvation must therefore be divided into at least two questions: "Who or what is the source of saving power?" and, "Who is being transformed by this power?" The biblical witness affirms that God alone, the Abba and Spirit of Jesus, is the source of life, grace, compassion, forgiveness, and the new creation. The God concretized in Jesus is the ground for faith and hope in the midst of evil, chaos and absurdity. God alone creates and transforms, and humans are called to be open or receptive to this saving power. This openness in the presence of Jesus becomes faith or trust in Jesus Christ. There is a radically new life in Christ. "There is a new creation; everything old has passed away; see, everything has become new" (II Cor. 5:17b). This same openness in the midst of the world religions where Jesus is absent, hidden or distorted may become a response to the Heart of the universe manifest in other cultural and religious forms. These forms may have their own mysterious depths and means of adoration; however, the disciples of Jesus immediately recognize the Mystery whenever the naked are clothed, the hungry fed, the marginalized center-staged, the hopeless comforted, the damned forgiven, and communities of compassion appear.

Like Jesus, Paul and his followers saw God's saving power in Christ universally active. In Romans 2:14-16, Gentiles who know the will of God as it is seared into their conscience may be excused, forgiven, on the day of judgment. In II Corinthians 5:16-24, Ephesians 1:3-13, and Colossians 1:15-23, Paul and Pauline theologians see God reconciling the whole of the totality into one unified cosmos in Christ. In I Peter 3:19, Christ's saving power is seen even in the realm of the dead.

Early Christians claimed the truth of the creative and saving Logos wherever the good, the true and the beautiful appeared. Justin Martyr, Clement of Alexandria and Augustine are striking examples of this universal theme.[39] In the third century, Origen wrote not only that the Logos is universally present, but that the power of Christ's cross heals and restores all reality.

> But we maintain that the power of Christ's cross and of his death... is so great, that it will be sufficient for the healing and restoration not only of the present and future ages, but even for those of the past, and not only for this human order of which we are a part, but even for the order of heavenly beings.[40]

With few exceptions, this universal theme moved into the dim background during the Middle Ages. However, it continued to be present within the Roman Catholic tradition and reemerged at the time of Vatican II.[41] Karl Rahner and Hans Küng have been powerful spokespersons for this vision within the Catholic tradition. Several contemporary Lutheran theologians including Wolfhart Pannenberg and Carl Braaten have also reclaimed the universal saving significance of God's power manifest in Christ. Both insist that God is at work throughout the whole of life and history. God's universal transforming work, identified in the resurrection of Christ, has saving significance for the whole of creation, history and the whole human family, not just for those who hear and respond to the gospel.[42]

A missiology for the 21st century will reaffirm this universal theme as a dimension of the Good News. *The finality of Jesus is confessed within God's universal and saving power, not in contradiction to it.* Jesus Crucified, the Christ, reveals and for all times and places defines what is the heart of our pulsating universe, the Abba of Jesus, who through the Spirit raised the vulnerable Messiah from the dead. The God of this grace is not bound by the limitations of our knowledge, our faith, our message or our mission.

Faith trusts that this message may be proclaimed with integrity even within the 21st-century world in which we gradually are becoming aware of a fifty billion-light-year universe. Faith trusts that the Heart of the universe will never be other than the breadth and depth of vulnerable, suffering love that came to expression and became concrete in Jesus.[43] This divine metacosmic love affirms and embraces all creation and enters the deserts and deepest hells of every rebellious cosmos in order that life may be nourished and transformed. Only crucified Truth is able to transcend the many truths of the universe. Such creation-affirming and suffering love may be universalized and absolutized, for it is the only power that does not threaten authentic life but allows it to bubble forth as springs in the desert!

## CHAPTER 2

# An Apology
# for a Reconstructed Missiology of the Cross:
## A Dialogue with Gerhard Forde's Presentation
### of Luther's Theology of the Cross

The contextualization of the theology of the cross for the purpose of witness and service in the 21st century is compelled to move beyond Luther's focus on personal salvation. Moving beyond personal salvation does not mean that the personal is not significant; however, other realities must be addressed. The 21st century demands that theology be thought within billions of cosmic light-years and the haunting possibility that our reality is ultimately a nanosecond of cosmic absurdity. A 21st-century theology of the cross must be reconstructed to address the world of religious pluralism and the tragic identification of the cross with Western Christendom and imperialism. It must include the conversation of women and the whole global Christian family. Global Christianity—witnessing and serving within a world marked by the horrendous gap between the haves and the have-nothings, the powerful and the vulnerable—is called by the Abba and Spirit of Jesus into solidarity with the pain and suffering of the world. Global Christianity calls for participation in a new creation.

## Forde's Interpretation of Luther

Gerhard O. Forde, a well-known interpreter of Luther's theology of the cross, argues against theological initiatives that seek to reconstruct and expand a theology of the cross for a post-Constantinian Christian century. For example, he argues powerfully against a vision of the suffering of a vulnerable God in and for the world. A conversation with Forde may clarify a number of issues that are at stake in this reconstruction of a theology of the cross.

In 1997 Forde published *On Being a Theologian of the Cross*, a concise explication of Luther's understanding of the theology of the cross. Forde explains Luther's thought through a study of The Heidelberg Disputation, Theses #1-28. In a 1965 report on the LWF discussions (1958-1962) on the meaning of justification, Jüng Rothermundt wrote:

> According to Reformation teaching, there is no way to salvation without the experience of a terrified conscience, without the acknowledgement of sin and the fueling of God's wrath. Justification is received as a comfort for the terrified conscience. Here, without doubt, a part of Luther's spiritual biography has entered into the dogmatic formulation. Is this not problematic? And does it not bring us into terrible embarrassment in face of the normal folk-church situation?[44]

Forde would reply to these questions with a resounding "no." "No," Luther's personal experience of the terrified conscience is not problematic for theology, because it describes the very heart of the God-human relationship. The terrified conscience is God's means of salvation. God, in God's alien work, kills, destroys, annihilates the sinner in order that new life may be created and spring forth, which is God's proper work.[45] Furthermore, for Forde, this expression of God's saving work is not an embarrassment. It should not have been in the folk-church of Europe, nor is it in the contemporary 21st-century U.S. context. In both contexts, the gospel has been distorted as Christianity is conformed to the values of contemporary society rather than those of the gospel. Forde particularly attacks what he describes as the sentimentality of contemporary theology where everyone becomes a suffering victim rather than a guilt-ridden sinner, where God becomes a sentimentally attractive God who identifies with us as victims in our pain rather than a terrifying Power that attacks and destroys the sinner in order to create new life. According to Forde, salvation is death, then resurrection. Forde describes the theological theme of his adversaries as "misery loves company."[46]

There is no question that Forde has described Luther's theology of the cross correctly. Luther identified the supreme heresy of the church as the belief that salvation is achieved by good works. Sin is a human Promethean attempt to storm heaven. Therefore, any positive action by the self must be examined intensely to avoid any attempt to self-justify in the presence of God. From Luther's perspective this self-justification is inevitable. Luther writes in Thesis 21, "It is impossible for a person not to be puffed up by his good works unless he has first been deflated and destroyed by suffering and evil, until he knows that he is worthless and his works are not his but God's."[47]

God's cross message is God's weapon for deflating, destroying, annihilating (Thesis 24) the self-justifying sinner. In Forde's terms, "[God's] cross attacks and afflicts us.... God himself does himself to us."[48] "The sinner neither knows nor speaks the truth about God and consequently can only be put to death by the action of God."[49] "'Thou shalt break them with a rod of iron' gives a good picture of the kind of suffering Luther has in mind."[50] This, says Forde, is how one becomes a theologian of the cross.

Luther and Forde assert that the cross is suffering. God wishes to be recognized in suffering.[51] Luther asserted that suffering is first, Christ's indescribable suffering as Christ suffers to appease the wrath of God.[52] The sinner, recognizing that this divine suffering is necessary because of his/her own sin and guilt, is crushed by a terror-stricken heart and a despairing conscience. This is the suffering imposed by God resulting in the annihilation that makes new life possible. Luther states in a sermon, "Here the passion of Christ performs its natural and noble work, strangling the old Adam and banishing all joy, delight and confidence which man could derive from other creatures, even as Christ was forsaken by God."[53] Luther is totally aware of the fact that the experience of God's terrifying wrath is experienced as the possibility of God abandoning us and not keeping God's word. Forde quotes Luther's seemingly strange words, "God cannot be God unless he first becomes a devil."[54]

Death makes new life/resurrection possible. This new life comes to expression in the life of faith. Self-justification is killed; justification by faith is raised. From this God-created miracle flow love and good works. "This is the love of the cross, born of the cross, which turns in the direction where it does not find good which it may enjoy, but *where it may confer* good upon the bad and needy person (Thesis 28)" (emphasis added).[55]

Unquestionably, Luther's theology of the cross springs from Luther's own intense spiritual experience.[56] The terrifying fear of the wrath of God was Luther's own experience as he vainly fought to justify himself in the presence of a medieval vision of a terrifying God. Within that terrifying fear (*Anfechtung*) Luther found a gracious vision of God, who through faith in Jesus Christ, granted justification of the sinner, the forgiveness of sin. To some within the Lutheran community, such as Forde, this vision of salvation is a wondrous gift. And this gift is still received as one encounters God's alien work in the form of a terrified conscience, the annihilation of the sinful self, and then resurrection in faith from the dead.

Forde's Annihilator belongs to an alien theological and spiritual world for many contemporary Christians. God is not experienced by everyone as the terrifying devil-God in the cosmic attic, and sin is not experienced as storming heaven. Rather, for many believers, God may be experienced as the awesome, overwhelming mystery of multiple Big-Bang cosmic constructs similar to our universe in which we are meaningless, minuscule participants in trillions of light-years of space. There is no cosmic attic to storm here. Instead, the question is whether we are simply caught in a nanosecond of cosmic absurdity. Faith within this vision of reality trusts that life ultimately is not tragic absurdity but that God has created life, human community, and human stewardship. The human adventure is a wondrous, miraculous mystery of life. Sin is blindness to the God-given design within the web of life. Sin is the refusal of humanity to weave its own existence in harmony with the cosmic design and the insistence to weave its own egocentric, destructive dreams into the web envisioned by the Cosmic Weaver. Awesome wonder within the possibility of cosmic absurdity is the reality for many of us. It is no longer even conceivable that one could dream of storming heaven in order to catch the attention of the demon-God in the attic.

When one realizes that the earth is but a tiny blue dot floating within trillions of light-years of space, grace begins not within the dialogue between sin and grace but within the dialogue between absurdity and grace. Sin is not experienced as the Promethean charge up the attic steps. Sin is the humiliating recognition that we are participants in destroying the gift of the Cosmic Weaver's web of life. Jesus' own familiar images—a shepherd searching for lost sheep, an aging father throwing all decorum aside to race down a rocky road in order to embrace a lost son, a Messiah who weeps over a nation walking to its own destruction, a prophet who warns that violence reaps violence and that a Zionist revolutionary dream will result in destruction and death for women and children, a prophet who denounces the powerful and rich for decimating the oppressed and tearing to shreds the web of life, the suffering servant of God who embraces the weak, sick, damned, and marginalized and places them around the messianic banquet table—these are images that are more significant for many than the Annihilator of Luther's and Forde's theological reflection. Since the Crucified Jesus—spiked to a cross, arms stretched wide, spoke words of forgiveness for the enemy in the midst of tortured pain—actually identifies God, one might trust that the Cosmic Mother with tears embraces the universe.

A similar critique comes from feminist and liberation theologians who experience another side of human brokenness. Sin is not experienced as pride storming up the cosmic stairs but as the devaluation of the self. Brokenness is the consciousness of having no self-value and no possibilities as the self, which results in fear of failure, the unwillingness to explore and venture, the willingness to be disregarded and denied a role in the cosmic web of life. Grace within this experience of emptiness is an encounter of acceptance and affirmation. It is the divine promise that you too are a child of the cosmic weaver and web and have value and potential that you have yet not dreamed of.[57]

### Forde's Failure to Understand His Adversaries

Theological images and symbols are rooted in our biographical histories, our religious experience, our culture. In Forde's case, he ultimately moves with Luther through the terror of annihilation and receives grace and life. What disturbs me about Forde's exposition is not so much his own exposition of Luther's theology of the cross, but his incapacity to understand what is being affirmed by his theological adversaries, the sentimentalizers of the cross.[58]

## Sentimentalizers of the Cross

Forde asserts that one of the reasons he writes the book is that the theology of the cross has become sentimentalized, "especially in an age that is so concerned about victimization."[59]

> Jesus is one who is spoken of as the one who "identifies with us in our suffering," or the one who "enters into solidarity with us" in our misery. "The suffering of God," or the vulnerability of God and such platitudes become the stock-in-trade of preachers and theologians who want to stroke the psyche of today's religionists. But this results in rather blatant and suffocating sentimentality. God is supposed to be more attractive to us because he identifies with us in our suffering. "Misery loves company" becomes the unspoken motif of such theology."[60]

It is quite obvious to many within the contemporary theological world, including myself, that there is a tradition within the biblical world that takes victims and victimization much more seriously than Forde does. In the Exodus story, God sees the affliction of God's people, hears their cries and knows (participates in) their suffering (Exod. 3:7). Jeremiah speaks movingly of God who weeps and wails because of the devastation of Israel where there is no longer even the lowing of cattle and where there are no longer birds and animals in the land (Jer. 9:10). Jesus weeps over Jerusalem as her people walk to their self-destruction (Luke. 19:41-44). The coming Son of Man is identified with the hungry, the thirsty, the imprisoned, the naked (Matt. 25:31ff.). The stories of Jesus in the Gospels often say that Jesus had compassion upon people, that is, shared their suffering. In both the Hebrew and Greek languages there are words that have been translated as "compassion," that is "agonizing with." In both cases a figure of speech is used that speaks of inner pain, like the twisting of the intestines or the pains of a woman in labor. This inner suffering is an expression of love for someone else who is in pain.[61] The theological insight that God becomes flesh (the incarnation of God) and identifies with human existence in all of its brokenness in order to transform all of life is the culminating affirmation of this Christian faith. Only theological insensitivity can trivialize this sacred story with the phrase "misery loves company."

This vision of God's solidarity with human suffering does not ring like sentimentality to those who experience life's brokenness, pain and death. Nearly one billion people live between life and death every day of their lives because of a lack of adequate diet and health care. Thirty thousand children die daily because they live within that world. Thirteen million orphans populate the African continent because AIDS has taken their parents away from them. The life expectancy in several African countries now approaches only thirty years. Palestinian youth confined to prisons or refugee camps live with a burning rage in their lives that tortures them every hour of the day. Six million Jews, many of them children, were thrown into fiery furnaces, and many asked, along with Elie Wiesel, "Where is God?"[62] This list could fill thousands of volumes, many that could be written within our own country and about our own people, people who may not be physically broken but are psychologically tormented. This reality should not be relegated to the penultimate of theology while the ultimate question is that of my or our salvation.[63]

In the 1980s, I was traveling in Namibia at a time when the South African apartheid system had a stranglehold on the black population. After a worship service, the pastor asked all those who had been in prison, all those who had children who were in prison, and those who had fled for their lives to please stand up. Half of the congregation of six hundred people stood. A visitor asked, "What keeps you going?" Their answer: "We trust that God is with us and for us." This is not a sentimentality that distorts the image of Luther's "devil God" who is intent on annihilating our ego. Rather, it is the vision of God whose love is so deep that God wills to share the pain and suffering of tortured lives.

This vision of the pain-love of God is a vision that has encircled the world. The center of the Christian world has moved south on the globe, and is most alive in those regions of the world that experience the most physical deprivation. As scripture is read in the midst of oppression and suffering, the church recaptures a prophetic theme. God shares the suffering of God's people and wills to transform life.

Faith holds on to that promise when everything in life and history seems to deny that promise. "We trust that God is with us and for us!"

## From Guilt to Victimization

A second reason for Forde's critique of the sentimentalizers of theology is that there has been a reversal in understanding the human condition. Once there was a focus upon human guilt and human sinfulness, but now humans are primarily victims. "Guilt places the blame on sinners."[64] Since we are now victims, caught in meaninglessness (rather than guilt), "everything is permitted and nothing is forgiven."[65]

I do not fault Forde for being concerned about human responsibility and guilt. Guilt implies a call to responsibility. Within the faith context, it implies being called by God into responsibility for human life and human community. Guilt is the awareness that one is not in conformity with the will and mission of God. As a responsible Lutheran, Forde would speak of the will of God in terms of the law, which from the Lutheran perspective is reflected in the commandments of God ultimately reducible to two: You shall love God and love your neighbor. Further reflection reduces these to one: Love God, who loves all creation and all people. To worship the God of biblical faith is to fall awestruck before the mystery that God, the beating Heart of the universe, loves creation and people. To love the God and Abba of Jesus is to love God who so loved the world. One cannot respond to that God without responding to the world, without taking responsibility for the world and neighbor. Furthermore, one cannot respond to the neighbor without consciously or unconsciously responding to God (Matt. 25:31ff. and I John. 4:7-10). The two commandments are integrally one and are inseparable. Guilt is one's awareness that one has not authentically responded to the brokenness and pain of the world which God loves and calls God's people to love.

Repentance is a total reversal of this irresponsibility, a reversal from not loving God and all of creation to responsible care of God's creation and all humanity. Repentance is a reversal from not trusting the God who is compassionately concerned about all of reality to trusting this same God, the Abba of Jesus and the Abba of the universe.

Forde separates ultimate redemption from a penultimate concern for caring for "the well being of persons in this age."[66] In Forde's theological world, the God who annihilates the self-justifying human in order that the justified human might come to life is separated from the God who passionately calls for justice-seeking in the world. Thus Forde can raise a cry for annihilation of the self for salvation's sake and at the same time make a few side comments about the penultimate concern for those who are burning in the hell of human existence. Furthermore, Dietrich Bonhoeffer's remarkable statement that "being a Christian is not being particularly religious, but participating in the suffering of God in the world" would need to be classified as an expression of that sentimentality. Forde writes, "'Misery loves company' is the prime theological motif. Christ humbled himself and descended into the world of suffering so we ought to too. If, on occasion this causes a bit of pain or discomfort, we can tally it up on our ledger of good works."[67] I suspect that it is a theological world molded by 17th-century Lutheran orthodoxy that makes it possible for Forde to make this statement and then to write:

> When penultimate cares are mistaken for ultimate redemption..., the church becomes predominantly a support group rather than the gathering of the body of Christ when the word of the cross and resurrection is proclaimed and heard.[68]

One wonders how Forde squares this trivialization of concern for those who suffer spiritually, psychologically and physically with Jesus' life and message. For example, the description of the last judgment in Matthew 25:31ff. reflects the biblical and prophetic concern for those who live in the world's hell. Passionate concern for the hungry, thirsty, naked, and imprisoned is a response of love to the creation and through the least in creation to God. The call to responsibility is a call to God who loves even the least. My response to Forde's comment about the church as a support group is that our call from God might be to participate in the "cosmic support group." A Trinitarian community through a new creation of human community miraculously and unknowingly becomes the cosmic support group of all those who live in the isolated and communal hells of the world. Think of the untapped potential power of support! Would that there were more cosmic support groups in reality.

From the biblical perspective, this is not an insignificant dimension of God's passion, but an integral dimension of the ultimate intention of God for humanity. Guilt is an awareness of the brokenness of our response to God's presence and mission in the world. God's call to faith and trust is a power that turns life around. The self-centered life, which does not wish or dream that it is possible to participate in God's vision of a new creation for all, is, in Luther's words, drowned, and the God-in-Christ–centered life is newly created. The new justified and Holy-Spirit–empowered self becomes a participant in God's passionate concern for the brokenness of the world.

God, repentance and faith are not realities that are hidden within some monadic, self-centered bubble but are realities within the interdependent cosmic web of life. In the web of life, God's passion for the transformation of the individual person is one aspect of God's passion for the transformation of the whole. God is passionately concerned about the world. Sin is not the Greek Prometheus storming the cosmic attic to steal fire. Rather, *sin is humanity's refusal to accept from God the stewardship of God's family and God's cosmic home in which the family dwells.* God's wrath doesn't burn because humanity does not tremble in God's presence. God's wrath—or tears—burn because God's children do not participate in God's design for family relationships, which when broken result in destruction of family and self. Forde separates the God-human relationship from the human-human relationships. Those relationships cannot be separated within the web of Life. This is a both-and, not an either-or, relationship. Forde can be critiqued for violating the both-and of healthy Lutheran theology with the either-or of a rationalistic orthodoxy.[69]

## Judgment Rather than Evil

Third, Forde also has a problem with contemporary theologians who "talk much about the problem of evil" and suffering, and neglect the Annihilator God who is the source of suffering.[70] One of the problems, which Forde rightly identifies, is that suffering is usually categorized as evil. Forde recognizes that evil may cause suffering, but that this is not necessarily the case. There are other sources of suffering, and Forde is correct in recognizing this fact, particularly when he writes, "love can cause suffering."[71] Suffering often indicates that something is out of order within God's creation, particularly within the moral order of God's design for life. Sin as ego-centered selves, ethnic groups, institutions or political realities that contradict God-intended community results in the demonic consequences of estrangement, irresponsibility, exploitation, human devastation, pain and suffering. Authentic love is love that is so deep that it is pained by the suffering of those who are loved. Love or compassion participates in the suffering of the beloved. It is in this sense that God shares the suffering of the world. It is in this sense that Bonhoeffer can write that "to be a Christian is not to be particularly religious but to share the suffering of God in the world."[72] Forde is correct in recognizing that love causes suffering; however, at the same time it must be emphasized that evil causes suffering. Evil is that reality, embodied in persons and societal structures, which contradicts God's intentions for the world and desecrates and destroys God's design of community, resulting in horrendous consequences for humanity and all of life.

The biblical faith is always aware of the continual conflict raging between the reign of God and the reign of Satan or evil. It is aware of the devastating consequences of evil's reign and the suffering and pain that result. The biblical world is also aware of the suffering-love of God, which, for the purpose of transforming life, is identified with the pain of the victims of Satan's assault on life.[73]

Theological reflection deals with a very complex question when attempting to understand what attacks life, what causes suffering and pain. On the one hand, suffering sometimes is described as the consequence of evil/Satan and at other times the judgment/wrath of God. The Deuteronomist of the Old Testament sees prosperity as the consequence of obedience to God and national humiliation and defeat as the judgment of God (Deut. 6:10-19). The book of Hebrews considers the suffering of persecution as not only the consequence of evil power but the discipline of God (Heb. 12:1-11). The book of Job is a debate as to whether suffering and pain are the consequence of sinful disobedience or not. Job concludes with a vision of God that powerfully proclaims that humans are not in a position to answer the ultimate questions of life's mysteries. Jesus rejects the simple identification of disease and disaster with the judgment of God. In

John 9, Jesus rejects the notion that a man was born blind because of his or his parents' sin. In Luke 13:1-5, Jesus rejects the idea that death by accident or by political persecution is the judgment of God. On the other hand, Jesus sees the suicidal Zionist walk of his own people as resulting in the judgment of God (Mark 13).

One finds the same ambiguity in Luther. In his book dealing with the invasion of Europe by the Turks, Luther sees the Turks as both an evil empire and as agents of the judgment/wrath of God. Both the Turks and God were the enemy outside the gates of Vienna. In other writings, a child's death may be the work of the devil[74] or the wrath of God.[75]

Forde and others within Lutheran orthodoxy tend to lose the ambiguity between evil and God's wrath by minimizing evil within the theological discussion in order to emphasize the role of the judgment and the wrath of God. I believe that this can lead to devastating descriptions of the nature of God. An unforgettable experience within my own life was a heated discussion on the Holocaust. I had made the statement that the only place to find God in the midst of burning flesh in cremation ovens was in the midst of the flames, in solidarity and identification with the screaming victims. An orthodox Lutheran theologian added, "Perhaps God is also fanning the flames." In other words, perhaps God's wrath is present in the demonic attack of Hitler and his Nazi cohorts. I refuse to put the Abba and Spirit of Jesus as causal agents into every experience of pain, suffering and destruction. Luther, however, seems to have no difficulty in seeing Jewish suffering as God's judgment. Luther can quite bluntly say that the desperation of the Jews, under attack for centuries by Christendom, is the consequence of the silence of God's wrath.[76]

In a recent lecture, another Lutheran orthodox theologian simply identified the attacks on the Twin Towers and the Pentagon of September 11, 2001, as the judgment of God. He did not note the ambiguity that it was also the result of evil. In further conversation he argued that it was God who destroyed the Twin Towers since everything that happens is God's will. He thought that he could ground this affirmation in Luther's discussion of the bondage of the will.[77]

The rage behind the September 11 attack may have had some of its roots in American arrogance and power. From that perspective, America reaps what it sows. As Abraham Lincoln observed in his second inaugural address:

> Fondly do we hope—fervently do we pray—that this mighty scourge of war may speedily pass away. Yet, if God wills that it continue, until all the wealth piled by the bondman's two hundred and fifty years of unrequited toil shall be sunk, and until every drop of blood drawn with the cash, shall be paid by another drawn with the sword, as was said three thousand years ago, so still it must be said: "the judgments of the Lord are true and righteous altogether."[78]

With scripture and tradition, we can at times speak of consequences as the judgment of God. Break the laws of the moral order of the universe and they will eventually break you.

However, the events of September 11 are also the consequences of evil forces. Not only the actions of the United States, interpreted as demonic, led to that attack, but also the demonic agents who so readily and devoutly flew airplane missiles loaded with human lives into buildings filled with human life. Theologically, evil as embodied in persons and social-political structures is a reality that has devastating consequences for human life. To minimize this reality and dramatize all suffering and destruction as God's judgment is to demonize God. God, who in love shares the pain of the world, is sacrificed on the altar of the Annihilator God who brings life out of death.

### The Vulnerability of God

According to Forde, a fourth platitude offered by the sentimentalizers of the gospel is the term "the vulnerability of God." Orthodox Lutheran theology is uncomfortable with vulnerability. God is the omnipotent, irresistible superpower within the universe. Justification is made possible when the cosmic irresistible power attacks the sinner with the gospel of the Crucified One. The sword of the Word, using a terrified conscience and suffering, drives the sinner to the foot of the cross in order that there might be a new creation, a new resurrection life.

Forde, like Martin Luther in "The Heidelberg Disputation," Theses 13-18, asserts that humans have no "free will."

They live in bondage to sin, curved in upon themselves. Release from that bondage is a creative act of the omnipotent, irresistible God. God destroys the sinful self; God creates faith; God makes the new creation possible.[79]

This theological move is rather parodoxical. On the one hand, Luther portrays God as being hidden and revealed in the Crucified. We see only the backside of God, because God comes to us in the form of the vulnerable baby Jesus who eventually is crucified. Christ shares the darkness and the despair of life. Through the Crucified, the sinner receives new life in the form of grace, forgiveness, justification and the life of the Spirit. This is the authentic vision that has the power to speak in a world of pain and absurdity. However, on the other hand, Luther and Forde speak of the "hidden God" in a deeper and more troubling sense. God ultimately is truly unknown. God is the *Deus absconditus*, the hidden God. There is a hidden God behind the God incarnate in the Crucified. There is the omnipotent, irresistible God who elects or predestines persons to be annihilated and justified in Christ. There are others in whom God wills not to create faith who are, therefore, destined for humanity's earned damnation. Luther makes a distinction between the Christ who is to be preached and the God who, though terrifying, is not to be questioned.[80] This vision no longer is love that will not let us go. The sheer grace that is hidden/revealed in the Crucified is sacrificed on the altar to the inscrutable will of the cosmic Lord. According to Alister McGrath and Kurt Hendel, this is an invalid interpretation of the gospel.[81] From the perspective of this writer, there is no God other than the God embodied and identified in the Crucified. There is no Hellenistic omnipotent power hidden behind the vulnerable God enfleshed in the Crucified. Tragically, Luther and Forde, who so vehemently insist upon God's revelation in Jesus Christ, betray that gospel to a Hellenistic philosophical rationalism, which they claim to unconditionally reject.

Within the world of pain and absurdity and the many truths of religious pluralism it is essential to affirm the biblical vision fulfilled in Jesus. It is the vision of the vulnerable, suffering, saving, transforming God that is able to address and transform life to be in conformity with the crucified and risen Christ. This vision, through the Spirit, has power to transform contemporary humanity marked by alienation, brokenness, enmity and the madness of violence and death. This vision challenges all forms of religious, theological and Christian "imperialism." This vision witnesses to Jesus Crucified, who came not to be served, but to serve and give his life as a ransom (a means of freedom) for many (Mark 10:45).

Forde's is a challenging voice. He has continually called the church to a gospel that focuses on grace, justification and forgiveness as sheer gift. *On Being a Theologian of the Cross* articulates that gospel for a context dominated by a terrifying God, where sin is arrogance and pride. A terrifying God and a terrified conscience still are an experienced reality for many people; however, this is not the reality for others. The dialogue between grace and absurdity is for many the crisis of a post-Christian century. For others, the dialogue between sin and grace is a dialogue between personal self-devaluation and grace's affirmation of personal worth and potential. Furthermore, Forde's vision is not the essential reality for millions who do not so much believe in a future hell as live in a terrifying contemporary hell on earth. Forde chooses to address this reality as less than ultimately significant. I believe that this is a serious gap in Forde's thought and in much of Lutheran orthodoxy. There are glimpses of another side of Forde's thought found in side comments and footnotes as noted above. Forde actually concludes his section on the discussion of the Christian life in Volume 2 of *The Church Dogmatics* with these words:

> The Christian vision leads into the world, to suffering for and with others in the expectation of God's will being done on earth as it is in heaven. The aim is not to gain one's own holiness or to bring in the kingdom by force or tyranny, but to care for God's creatures and God's creation.[82]

The primary thesis of this chapter is that the "suffering-with" of the body of Christ flows from the suffering-with-us God. Once again, to be a Christian is to share the suffering of God in the world.

## CHAPTER 3

# Religious Pluralism:

## Exploring Options for New Relationships

Religious pluralism and interfaith relationships are increasingly facts of life for our own culture and society. Previous generations experienced religious pluralism as a distant reality separated by oceans and involving alien cultures. Today, immigration patterns, international political realities, and developments in communication technology have placed religious pluralism at our doorstep. Interfaith relationships are no longer relegated to international specialists but are the possibility and responsibility of us all.

September 11, 2001, created a tremendous interest in world religions, particularly Islam. For some, Islam represents a false or demonic religion. For others, Islam represents a religious community grounded in deep moral values which at one point in history (9th and 10th centuries A.D.) represented the best in world civilization. How do we begin to understand the variety of Christian responses to religious diversity? The purpose of this chapter is to describe and respond to a number of theological models that express various understandings of how Christians relate to the religious "other." This theological journey may enable us to explore our own attitudes and perspectives and thereby inform our own interfaith journey as we are called to participate in the *Missio Dei.*

## Religious Pluralism

Religious pluralism is a sociological fact. There are approximately 2.2 billion Christians around the globe, 1.1 billion Muslims, 800 million Hindus, 350 million Buddhists, 1 billion secularists, 100 million Traditionalists, and many others, including 13 million Jews. Within the city of Chicago there are 350,000 Muslims, 80,000 Hindus, 220,000 Buddhists, and 220,000 Jews. Religious pluralism is increasingly a reality in all our communities. Our doctor may be an Indian Hindu, our children may play soccer with Muslim children, the local banker may be a Buddhist.[83]

Religious pluralism is not simply a sociological fact. It is experienced by the pluralistic community from a variety of perspectives. For some people, religious pluralism makes a positive contribution to their community. New values, new insights, new experiences, and new relationships add color to the multicolored tapestry that is the religiously plural community. For others religious pluralism is a threat to the community. Diverse religious commitments are seen as undermining the stability of society or as a threat to national security. This has been particularly evident in the U.S. after September 11. Many U.S. citizens understand the U.S. to be a "Christian" country and find the presence of Muslims, Hindus and Buddhists a threat to national unity and security. Others understand "alien" religions to be demonic. A number of statements from evangelical fundamentalists, such as Franklin Graham and Jerry Falwell, reflect this fear of pluralism. For others there may be both a joy in finding a more inclusive human community and a wariness concerning the stability and security of the community and nation.

Discussions concerning interfaith relationships and dialogue seem inevitably to end in discussions about the "finality" or "normativity" of one faith's vision and the faith visions of other communities. For some, even to make a positive comment about another religious tradition or people is to some extent seen as a denial of one's own faith and tradition. The revelatory events of one's own faith are unique, absolute and final. This implies that one religion is superior and worthy of trust. Any positive statement about other religions may appear to threaten or undermine the faith foundation upon which we build our lives. Philosophical and theological relativism must be denied if faith is to be certain and secure.

Relativism, in contrast to ultimate truth, is a primary presupposition of what is designated postmodernism. Traditional orthodoxy found truth in the past in revelation, sacred scriptures and doctrine. Modernism rejected revelatory and ecclesiastical authority, claiming that the only authority was reason. Modernism assumed that reality was unified and rational and that truth therefore was discoverable by the human mind.

Postmodernism rejects both orthodoxy and modernism and their claims to final truth. For the postmodernist, all reality and knowledge of reality is a social construct. Human communities and cultures, through thought, intuition and imagination, create the worlds, the "sacred canopies," in which we live.[84] Each community, each culture is unique, being the consequence of a particular historical context and movement. Each culture, from its own time and place, has a particular perspective from which its people view their reality. Each community has its own particular criteria for truth, a truth that serves its members well or is denied. In a postmodern world there are multiple truths relative to each context. Claims to find one final religious truth are considered inappropriate, even absurd.

## Five Models for Understanding Interfaith Relationships

Generalization, and, in this case, interpretive models are always questionable, because they oversimplify and fail to capture the nuances made by particular perspectives. Nevertheless, models are helpful in interpreting a vast amount of material and making comparisons possible. In contemporary theological discussion three models are often used in interpreting the discussion concerning the relationships between Christianity and people of other faiths. They are exclusivism, inclusivism, and pluralism. Besides these three, this chapter will describe two other models, the correlational and the pluralism-of-salvation models.

### The Exclusivist Model

The Christian exclusivist is convinced that there is one final revelation of God and one ultimate saving event of God, namely Jesus Christ. There is one true, saving religion.

There is no revelation or saving activity of God in other religions. Salvation is not a possibility outside the preaching of Christ and faith in Jesus Christ. However, there may be glimpses of truth in other religions.

In the year 2000 at the invitation of Billy Graham ten thousand evangelical theologians, evangelists, mission strategists and church leaders from two hundred countries gathered to study, discuss and pray about the continuing task of world evangelization. Out of that meeting came "The Amsterdam Declaration." In this document, there is a brief statement on "Religious Pluralism and Evangelism" that illustrates Christian exclusivism. It reads:

> Today's evangelist is called to proclaim the gospel in an increasingly pluralist world. In this global village of competing faiths and many world religions, it is important that our evangelism is marked both by faithfulness to the good news of Christ and humility in our delivery of it. Because God's general revelation extends to all points of his creation, there may well be traces of truth, beauty and goodness in many non-Christian belief systems. But we have no warrant for regarding any of them as alternative gospels or separate roads to salvation. The only way to know God in peace, love and joy is through the reconciling death of Jesus Christ the risen Lord.[85]

An earlier section of the declaration places this statement within the context of Christ's judgment. "Therefore all human beings now face final condemnation by Christ the judge, and eternal destruction, separated from the presence of the Lord."[86]

There are a variety of theological positions within what is designated as exclusivism. There are fundamentalists who would deny traces of truth outside of Christ or claim that other religious expressions are demonic (Jerry Falwell). On the other hand there are persons sometimes categorized as exclusivists who believe that God's saving event, Christ, has saving implications beyond the preaching of the Gospel (Karl Barth). "The Amsterdam Declaration" expresses an exclusivist position that not only avoids the extremes within the model but represents the faith of millions of "Evangelical" Christians who are major voices within the United States.

### The Inclusivist Model

The inclusivist believes that Christ is God's normative revelation or God's universally saving event. However, in contrast to the exclusivist, God's revealing and saving power is present within all history and within every culture and people.

Inclusivism includes two types. The first can be described as the Inclusivist Representative Model. The Roman Catholic theologian Karl Rahner fits within this model. Rahner trusts that God, who is love, wishes all humanity to know salvation. In order to achieve this, God gives to all people what Rahner calls "the supernatural existential." This gift enables all humankind to be open or closed to the grace of God. Jesus is the final, ultimate revelation, because Jesus is the human who is fully open to the presence and saving power of God. In this Christ one sees that reality which is potentially a reality in every human being. Rahner sees the supernatural existential as a universal gift, and therefore God's grace may break through everywhere, even among other religions. "Every human being is really and truly exposed to the influence of divine, supernatural grace, which offers an interior union with God and by means of which God communicates himself whether the individual takes up an attitude of acceptance or refusal towards this grace."[87] Rahner is convinced that supernatural grace, at work within those open to grace, is found throughout human history and religions. This means for Rahner that "Christianity does not simply confront the members of extra-Christian religions as a mere non-Christian but as someone who can and might already be regarded in this or that respect as an anonymous Christian."[88] Jesus Christ is the normative expression of the saving God who is universally present to save and act within other religions. Grace comes to full expression in Jesus Christ.

Rahner's model is sometimes called the representative/expressive inclusivist model. The Roman Catholic theologian Hans Küng develops his thinking from Rahner's theological position. Following another Catholic theologian, Heinz Robert Schlette, Küng speaks of the world religions as God's ordinary means of salvation. The traditions, symbols, events, and words within religious communities have grown out of a people's openness to God's grace. Therefore God uses those gifts as means of transforming or saving people through God's grace. Christianity, however, is the extraordinary means of salvation because Christ is the fullest and normative expression of the grace. That normative faith will be shared by the church with all humanity.[89]

Pope John Paul II has not been enthusiastic about this development within Catholic theology and has rejected the terminology "ordinary" and extraordinary religion.[90] In the recent *Dominus Iesus*, the Vatican found it fitting to add this conditional statement: "If it is true that the followers of other religions can receive divine grace, it is also certain that 'objectively speaking' they are in a gravely deficient situation in comparison to those who, in the church, have the fullness of the means of salvation."[91]

A second type of inclusivism falls under the Inclusive Instrumental/Constitutive Model. This model articulates the view that Christ is God's final revelation and God's ultimate saving event. God not only comes to expression in Christ, but God does something new in this saving event, the effects of which may be understood as encompassing the whole of humanity and creation. What distinguishes this view from the exclusivist model is that there is a much greater appreciation for God's revelatory and saving activity outside the traditional house of faith. The Word or Logos of God, which became incarnate in Jesus Christ, is recognized as the Word of God that permeates all creation. Wherever wisdom, truth, love, justice, and beauty appear they are recognized as the "general" revelation of God. This general revelation appears under the cultural forms and patterns of all religions. The biblical traditions are replete with the identification of God outside the household of faith. Melchizidek, a Caananite priest of the Most High God, blessed Abraham (Gen. 14.18-20); Proverbs 8 recognized the presence of Wisdom, the co-creator of reality, as the source of justice among all the kings and nobles of the earth (Prov. 8.15-16). Paul recognizes the conscience seared into the fabric of humanity as the voice of God and concludes, "and their conflicting thoughts will accuse or perhaps excuse them on the day when, according to my gospel, God, through Jesus Christ, will judge the secret thoughts of all" (Romans 2:14-16). Jesus, in the parable of the last judgment in Matthew 25:31ff., states that humanity from all corners of the earth will be judged by how they responded to their neighbor in need, not knowing that the Son of Man is present, though hidden, there.

Some theologians would make further affirmations of God's revealing and saving work outside the household of faith. They would proclaim the Christ in order that people might be saved, but would also recognize that the saving work of God in Christ may very well incorporate people from outside the household of faith into God's kingdom. However, although they would hope for that inclusion through the saving act of God in Jesus Christ, they would leave the reality of that inclusion in the hands of God.[92]

Wolfhart Pannenberg and Carl Braaten develop a definite inclusive constitutive/instrumental model. They both see God as active within all of history and within every culture. All the religions of the world are traditions in which God is active. This biblical God is the God of the future in which all of cosmic life will be transformed and where righteousness, love, truth and justice will be realized. Since God is universally active, people within all religious traditions are, in a sense, the "footprints" of God within history.

However, Braaten and Pannenberg see Jesus Christ as not only the revealing event but the saving event within this historical process. Within the Jewish tradition, with its eschatological hopes, Jesus preaches the coming reign of God, the hope that all of life is and will be transformed. Within Jesus' mission he is crucified, but most significantly God raises Jesus from the dead. For Pannenberg, the resurrection is God's vindication of Jesus' mission and message. The future that Jesus proclaimed is guaranteed by God's raising Jesus. In Paul's terms, Jesus is the first "fruit" of those to be raised from the dead. In Braaten and Pannenberg's terms, God's future resurrection is now a present reality and identifies the future of all of history.

All religions moving toward God's future will eventually be incorporated into the eschatological future of God. Furthermore, Christians recognize the presence of God when they see the hungry fed, the naked clothed, the prisoners visited, and the thirsty given something to drink[93] and recognize that the present and hidden Son of Man is being responded to. Furthermore, this model makes clear that the saving activity of God in Christ will be universally effective in incorporating all of history within God's grace.[94]

The National Council of the Churches of Christ in the U.S.A. has incorporated both the exclusivist model and the inclusivist model into its statement, "Interfaith Relations and the Churches." One section of the document reads:

> Jesus Christ is also the focus of the most vexing questions regarding how Christians understand their relationship with men and women of other religions. Christians agree that God incarnated and incarnates still—the inexhaustible love and salvation that reconciles us all. We agree that it is not by any merit of our own, but by God's grace and our faithful response that we are reconciled. Likewise, Christians also agree that our discipleship impels us to become reconciled to the whole human family and to live in proper relationship to all God's creation. We disagree, however, on whether non-Christians may be reconciled to God, and if so, how. Many Christians see no possibility of reconciliation with God apart from a conscious acceptance of Jesus Christ as incarnate Son of God and personal savior [the exclusivist model]. For others, the reconciling work of Jesus is salvific in its own right, independent of any particular human response [an instrumental inclusivist model].[95]

### The Pluralist Model: Ramblings along the Rubicon

The exclusivist and inclusivist models have been challenged by the pluralist model, which insists that Christianity is meant to be not Christocentric but Theocentric. Theology is not centered in Christ but in the reality of God, particularly in a common experience of the mystery of God. Jesus Christ is one of many revealing and saving events that originate and spring forth from the one reality of God. Other religions are ways of salvation without reference to Christ. There is no normative Christology.

John Hick, formerly Professor of Philosophy of Religion at Claremont Graduate School in California, is widely recognized as a leading spokesperson of this model. Paul Knitter, a Catholic lay theologian, was another highly recognized advocate of this model. In 1985 Knitter published the now-famous volume *No Other Name? A Critical Survey of Christian Attitudes Toward the World Religions*[96] in which he offers an excellent survey of the various interfaith Christian models. Within that survey he argues for a theology committed to a non-normative Christology within what he designates as "unitive pluralism."

Knitter assumed that the reality of the one Mystery comes to expression in a variety of religious revelations and manifestations. Dialogue is needed to explore the Truth behind all religious truths, that is, a unitive pluralism. Both Knitter and Hick were convinced that the exclusivist and inclusivist models, with their assertion of the finality of Jesus Christ, resulted in Christian arrogance and imperialism that was divisive of humanity and made authentic dialogue between Christians and people of other faiths impossible. Furthermore, there were challenges from philosophy, psychology and the study of world religions that demanded a rethinking of the relationship between peoples of faith.

In 1987, Orbis Books published a volume in their "Faith Meets Faith" series titled *The Myth of Christian Uniqueness: Toward a Pluralistic Theology of Religions*.[97] The editors of the book were Hick and Knitter, and the essays emerged from a conference held at the Claremont Graduate School, Claremont, California, March 7-8, 1986. In the preface to the book, Knitter writes that the conference attempted to bring together people with new understandings of the relationship between Christianity and other religions:

> "New understandings" were described as any effort to move beyond the two general models that have dominated Christian attitudes towards other religions up to the present: the "conservative" exclusivist approach, which finds salvation only in Christ and little, if any, value elsewhere; and the "liberal" inclusivist attitude, which recognizes the salvific richness of other faiths but then views this richness as the result of Christ's redemptive work and as having to be fulfilled in Christ. We wanted to gather theologians who were exploring the possibilities of a pluralistic position—a move away from the insistence on the superiority or finality of Christ and the recognition of the independent validity of other ways. Such a move came to be described by participants in our project as the crossing of a theological Rubicon.[98]

Participants described this shift in theological perspective as a "monstrous shift" (Langdon Gilkey), a "fundamental revision" (Gordon Kaufmann), "genetic-like mutation" (Raimunds Panniker), "a momentous Kairos" (Knitter), a "Copernican revolution" and "radical transformation" (Hick)."[99]

It is interesting to note that the original crossing of the Rubicon from Gaul to Italy (north to south) in 49 B.C.E. by the General Julius Caesar was understood by the Roman Senate as an act of war. The Claremont gathering no doubt recognized that their assertion of a new pluralistic approach to interfaith relationships would be recognized by many within the Christian churches as an attack on the traditional faith. The Claremont gathering probably had visions similar to Julius Caesar of taking over the empire.

The essays in *The Myth of Christian Uniqueness* are divided into three bridges used to cross the theological Rubicon in challenging the traditional faith of Christian churches. First is the historic-cultural bridge of relativity. Cultural and historical relativism assumes that every cultural and historical expression or event is limited by and relative to a particular time and place. No event, truth, or revelation transcends this relativism and can be used to norm another event, truth, or revelation. "All of these diverse conceptions and pictures (from cultural and religious traditions) seem best understood as the product of human imaginative creativity in the face of the mystery that life is to all of us."[100]

Second is the theologic-mystical bridge of mystery. It would appear that one underlying, hidden, inner divine Mystery comes to expression in every religion. Every religion partially expresses this Mystery. Knitter writes, "The object or content of authentic religious experience is infinite—Mystery beyond all forms, exceeding our every grasp of it.[101]

Third is the ethico-practical bridge of justice. This third bridge to pluralism is not "a consciousness of historical relativity or absolute Mystery, but the confrontation with the suffering of humanity and the need to end such outrages."[102] The argument is that religious claims to superiority lead to attitudes of superiority resulting in conflict, domination, and exploitation. Rosemary Radford Ruether writes: [Christianity's] commandments of love and universal fellowship between people evidently have not served as a check on this internecine warfare. Crusades, witch-hunts, religious wars, and pogroms have all been a part of this violent, chauvinistic history of Christianity."[103] Justice and compassion are to be found in the renunciation of "finality" and the willingness of all religious communities to cooperate in overcoming the problems that produce poverty, violence and oppression.

These are the three bridges that lead to pluralism. From the perspective of more traditional understandings of inter-faith relationships, the bridges are seen as basic challenges to finality claims. Returning to the image of crossing the Rubicon, what Julius Caesar saw as tools (bridges) to challenge the power of the Roman Senate, the Senate saw as an act of war.

## An Inclusive Response to the Pluralist Model

In 1992, Orbis published another book in the "Faith Meets Faith" series titled *Christian Uniqueness Reconsidered: The Myth of a Pluralistic Theology of Religions*, edited by Gavin D'Costa. In a variety of ways the essays in this volume question and challenge the pluralistic model advocated in *The Myth of Christian Uniqueness*. D'Costa writes in the preface:

> One of the purposes of this book is to help indicate that the Rubicon is a deeper and more treacherous river than initially recognized. We have also wanted to show that there are many other creative, imaginative and socially sensitive ways in which Christian theology can proceed in its encounter with the world religions.[104]

Within the fourteen essays representative of the inclusive model, a number of challenges are made to the pluralist model. First, several authors question whether there actually is a common religious or psychological experience or one "Holy Other" lying behind the multiplicity of religious experiences within humanity. Furthermore, is it possible to separate the so-called inner kernel of religious experience from the cultural outer husks of that experience? Particularly in a postmodern world this question has legitimacy. The question is crucial for Knitter and Hick because their theological argument is based on the assumption that one ultimate Reality is the whence of all authentic religious experience.[105]

A second challenge to the pluralist model is that in its quest to make dialogue possible between peoples of faith it actually prevents dialogue from happening. For example, Christianity, Islam, and Buddhism all make claims to finality of Truth. True dialogue is possible when people are accepted and converse within their claims to finality. Several contributors argue that what pluralists actually do is create a new faith of "unitive pluralists." This new faith believes that one

Reality and one religious experience are common to all humanity. Critics of pluralism do not see "unitive pluralism" as a unifying, underlying religious experience that must be accepted before peoples of faith can dialogue with each other. The critics argue that it is more honest and helpful to accept our differences, including our different truth claims, and enter into dialogue with them. [106]

Third, a few authors point out that normative claims to finality do not necessarily lead to imperialistic, exploitive or oppressive attitudes and actions.[107] In my book *The Word and the Way of the Cross,* I argue that it should be quite the opposite. If Christians truly are conformed to the cruciformed mission of Christ, the way of the cross cannot be imperialistic but is rather the way of creative, suffering servanthood. To be great in the kingdom of God is to walk with and as the least within the story of the reign of God (Mark. 10:35-45).[108]

Fourth, a few critics state that the relativism within the pluralistic model may lead to ethical and moral chaos. Gilkey made this point in the earlier volume, *The Myth of Christian Uniqueness.* He noted that within the necessity of recognizing the place of relativity within culture and religion we are confronted by horrendous evil as, for example, in Nazi Germany. One recognizes immediately that in this confrontation one needs a rock (an absolute) upon which to stand in order to name and challenge the demonic powers that destroy life.[109] At the same time, there is a need for caution (a recognition of our relative perspective) lest we participate in an oppressive religious absolutism.

Fifth, many authors argue that Christianity cannot be understood apart from the claims to finality that are made for Jesus Christ in the New Testament. This is stated in response to pluralists who assert that the New Testament claims for Jesus' finality are relative to the context of first-century Christianity. The authors of *Christian Uniqueness Reconsidered* believe that Christianity should continue to make normative claims about Jesus Christ.

Within the critique of pluralism the authors share insights and make suggestions as to how the Christian community might go about relating to persons of other faiths. This essay does not explore those suggestions but follows the impact which this critique made on Knitter and the pluralist model and which led to two other interfaith models.

### Paul Knitter's Correlational Model

Knitter became the author of what he called the correlational model. The Orbis "Faith Meets Faith" series not only made possible this dialogue concerning interfaith relationships but also facilitated the emergence of the correlational model through its publication of three volumes that focused upon the work of Knitter: *The Uniqueness of Jesus: A Dialogue with Paul Knitter; One Earth Many Religions: Multifaith Dialogue and Global Responsibility;* and *Jesus and the Other Names: Christian Mission and Global Responsibility.*[110]

In concluding *One Earth Many Religions,* Knitter writes:

> I've tried to make a case that the best way to carry on a multifaith dialogue that will encourage all the participants to relate to each other in a conversation in which everyone genuinely speaks and listens to each other is to base such a dialogue on a shared commitment to promoting eco-human well being of Earth and Humanity.[111]

The statement indicates the direction in which Knitter's thought has turned.

First, Knitter increasingly focused his understanding of Jesus and Christianity on the pain and suffering of people and creation.[112] He speaks of moving from Christocentrism to Theocentrism and finally to soteriocentrism, which focuses upon the transformation of a suffering people and world, a movement to global responsibility.[113] As part of that move Knitter accepts the critics' challenge that dialogue cannot be rooted in the acceptance of a common experience of Mystery lying behind all religious phenomena. "Rather than presuppose a common core for all individually wrapped religious experience (since we cannot discard the wrapping), I am now following the lead of those who hold up 'salvation' or 'well-being' of humans and earth as the starting point."[114]

Second, Knitter speaks of a correlational model emphasizing the need of conversation, of listening, of relationships of receiving as well as giving, in which all participants are given equal rights and treated equally.[115]

At this point, Knitter has again listened to his critics. He has moved from insisting that dialogue must begin with an assumption of religious parity to an equal voice and place in the conversation.[116] Within the parameters of Knitter's concern for dialogue and global responsibility he develops the theological framework of his correlational model.

Knitter again has listened to his critics who challenged his earlier non-normative Christology as not only nonbiblical but irrelevant to a world in which moral evil is confronted. Knitter then develops a multi-normative approach to religious pluralism. In developing this approach, Knitter argues that the uniqueness of Jesus as the revelation of God is not that Jesus is the full, definitive and unsurpassable revelation of God but that Jesus is the universal, decisive and indispensable revelation of God. Jesus is not the full revelation, because this is not only idolatrous (identifying the finite and infinite) but limits God from revelation at other time and places. However, Jesus' revelation is universal in having meaning for people in all times and places. Furthermore, the revelation of God in Jesus is not definitive or unsurpassable since either category restricts/limits God. However, Jesus is decisive in that he shakes and challenges us, and Jesus is indispensable in that we need this revelation to be truly fulfilled. Knitter summarizes this perspective by saying Jesus is truly but not solely the revelation of God.[117] Knitter continues by noting that there is the probability that there may be other universal, decisive and indispensable revelations of God,[118] and Christians are to be open to being enriched within the process of interfaith relationships. However, Knitter is confident that these revelations will not contradict each other.[119]

Knitter was also impacted by fellow Catholic theologians who questioned the orthodoxy of his pluralistic approach. Responding to his critics, Knitter writes, "Christians must continue to proclaim Jesus as savior and divine. But what do these announcements mean? And how can Christians continue to make these proclamations in such a way that they maintain the uniqueness of Jesus without closing themselves to the uniqueness of other religious figures and revelations?"[120] Knitter believes that he can do this on the basis of a representational Christology rather than a constitutive Christology. In the latter, God does something new through Jesus Christ through whom salvation is realized, whereas in the representational Christology Jesus reveals something that is already universally present and active. Within the representational view Knitter can say that Jesus is savior and divine.[121]  In this sense Jesus is a primordial sacrament. Within this context Knitter can also say, "Then I can recognize that the love of God (revealed in Jesus) is broader than Jesus and can, perhaps, be revealed elsewhere in different but equally effective ways."[122]

With this discussion, Knitter emphasizes that within our contemporary context Jesus is to be primarily understood as an agent of the liberating kingdom of God.  In *The Uniqueness of Jesus* Knitter writes:

> The content of Jesus' uniqueness must be made
> clear in Christian life and witness.  This content,
> however, will be understood and proclaimed differ-
> ently in different contexts and periods of history.
> Today, the uniqueness of Jesus can be found in his
> insistence that salvation or the Reign of God must be
> realized in this world through human actions of love
> and justice.[123]

This is the basic thesis in Knitter's new approach to dialogue.  He writes, "Unless we are realizing salvation or well-being in and for this world we are not announcing the salvation announced by Jesus.  This is the unique ingredient in his saving message."[124]  Knitter was deeply moved by a visit to India in 1991 where he witnessed incredible poverty and suffering.  He has also been influenced by the Asian, Latin American and feminist theologians who, writing within the context of oppression and suffering, have been grasped by the biblical emphasis on liberation, justice and transformation of life.

Finally, it needs to be noted that Knitter understands his theological language concerning Christ to be performative or action language.  That is, to confess Jesus as Lord is to walk in discipleship in faithful obedience to Jesus' revelation of the Kingdom of God.

### A Response to Knitter's Correlational Model

Knitter can be appreciated for his capacity to listen and respond to theological positions that challenge his own theology.  His correlational model, from my perspective, is much more adequate than his original pluralistic model in *No Other Name?*  However, I still have several issues to raise.

Several writers have indicated that Knitter's criteria for the uniqueness of Jesus are very limited.  The criteria, to a large extent, are confined to Jesus' announcement of the kingdom of God active within history for the purpose of the transformation of history and life. This transformation results in justice and meaningful life for all. While fully appreciating the major significance of this approach and without minimizing the truth of this insight, it is also a fact that there are other dimensions of Jesus that contribute profoundly to his uniqueness and molding of the Christian faith. Another dimension is Jesus' spirituality as a Spirit-called, Spirit-empowered, Spirit-led, Spirit-possessed and eventually Spirit-raised person. Knitter's remarks concerning Jesus as a sacrament would indicate that he would be in agreement with this observation. Furthermore, from my Lutheran perspective, it must be clearly stated that Jesus' relationships with all people, whether marginalized, poor, condemned, oppressed, oppressor, or sinner, flowed from an absolutely unconditional love. This unconditional love made table fellowship with "sinners" not only possible but, from Jesus' perspective, a God-necessitated participation in the kingdom mission. This love also made unreliable, failing, deserting and betraying disciples candidates for missionary status within the body of Christ—instruments within the kingdom of God.

Again, from my own perspective it is also problematic when Knitter insists that the saving/revealing event of Jesus Christ is surpassable. Knitter does qualify this statement by saying that Christians are confident that other revelations will not contradict that which is incarnate in Jesus Christ. However, he so limits the criteria for Jesus' uniqueness and is so open to differences (for example, he does not seem to see any contradiction or incompatibility between the life visions of Christianity and Buddhism) that I, and many others, question whether this perspective might be vulnerable to losing powerful dimensions of the faith. I, for example, would insist that "unsurpassable" means that God will never be any other than the God concretized in Jesus Christ. God will never be other than Jesus' "Abba," who, in costly, pain-filled love, is passionately wrapped up in a broken and suffering world, who is even willing in God's self and through Jesus Christ to go through death and hell in order that forgiveness and new life might spring forth from death, and joy and hope might bubble forth from the desert of human existence. It is this love that embraces all reality, permeates all existence, makes all life possible, and is the source of God's revealing and saving presence and activity.

Finally, Knitter, as well as many other contemporary Christian theologians, has problems in working out his new theologies because of the manner in which he has reinterpreted the resurrection. Knitter makes it very clear in *No Other Name?* (see pp. 199-200) that he interprets the resurrection in terms of subjective/objective visions which have a transforming effect upon the early disciples. He states that this is similar to the way in which the Buddha has transformed the life of his followers. This interpretation does not adequately account for the experience of the early witnesses who reported in the New Testament an empty tomb and presence encounters. Nor does it account for the emerging theology of the cross, which places the darkness of Good Friday within the heart of God, or for the boldness and courage of the early disciples as they were tormented and crucified by the Romans.

### The Pluralism-of-Salvation Model

Professor S. Mark Heim in a 1995 volume, *Salvation: Truth and Difference in Religion* (also a "Faith Meets Faith" publication), develops a thorough critique of the pluralistic model. Heim's basic challenge is that pluralism, contrary to its own intent, does not take pluralism seriously. Pluralism does not truly accept the religious diversity within world religions but seeks a universal unifying religious reality beneath the surface of religious phenomena. Heim analyzes the work of three pluralists as he develops his own position. Hick presupposes one "Reality," one "Wholly Other," that comes to expression in a variety of faith expressions; Cantwell Smith finds one "faith attitude/orientation" behind a variety of faith expressions; and Knitter insists that all religions seek for a common "eco-human justice," which makes religious dialogue possible and effective.

Heim notes that these pluralists insist that interfaith dialogue and relationships are possible on the basis that one ignores the religious particulars and finds a unifying reality beneath the surface. Heim argues that this search for an abstract reality lying behind or below the particulars is a Western cultural product and that, for the pluralist, this abstract reality, not the actual religious expressions, represents religious truth.   This Western philosophical approach does not have to take particular religious traditions seriously.[125]

Dialogue is not a dialogue between particular religious perspectives but between those who recognize the "true reality" that unites humanity and the cosmos.  In his analysis, Heim notes the questionability of seeking to distinguish between religious phenomena and abstract reality[126] and also notes that what pluralists actually achieve is to create one more religious community among the world religions.[127]  We noted similar critiques in an earlier discussion. However, Heim is to be commended for the thoroughness of his argument.

In contrast to the pluralistic model, Heim seeks "to find a fruitful way of combining recognition of truth or validity and difference across religions.... A perspective is needed which can recognize the effective truth of what is truly other."[128]

Heim develops his appreciation for "the other" through a philosophical perspective advanced by Nicholas Rescher called "orientational pluralism."  In contrast to claims that there is one truth, no truth, or partial and complementary truths, Rescher claims that within our given reality all observations and assertions concerning that reality are made from a particular perspective.  Observers viewing from different perspectives see different things.  Their assertions may seem to conflict and contradict; however, their assertions may all be true from their various perspectives.[129]

Heim uses this insight to advocate for the validity of a legitimate religious diversity and the possibility of a variety of religious perspectives.  In seeking an hypothesis that may affirm most adequately the differences within religious traditions, Heim proposes that religious aims, fulfillments, or forms of salvation are varied. "In my view the key to such an effort [understanding religious pluralism] is an emphasis on the fulfillment of various religious ends."[130]

Heim argues that there is an organic, integral relationship between a religious perspective and practice with the end sought as fulfillment of life.  "There should be some integral relationship between future human states and present ones, else the universe is organized neither with the principles of equity we recognize nor with the processes of development we can conceive.  I agree with this conten-

tion."[131]  Heim goes on to state that different religious traditions affirm different religious goals.  Christians seek communion with the Triune God; Buddhists seek Nirvana.  Within
Heim's views of the multiplicity of perspectives the goals of
communion with the Triune God and Nirvana are not contra-
dictory.  "True, they cannot both be true at the same time for
the same person.  But for different people, or the same person
at different times, there is no necessary contradiction in both
being true."[132]  Heim argues that a diversity of religious goals
(salvation) is the case for humanity within the historical plane
but also for post-death experience if this be the reality.[133]
Because a variety of human fulfillments are possible, Heim
writes, "I suggest that Christians can consistently recognize
that some traditions encompass religious ends which are
states of human transformation, distinct from that Christians
seek.... The crucial question among the faiths is not 'which
one saves?' but 'what counts as salvation?'"[134]

From Heim's Christian Trinitarian perspective, he sees
the multiplicity of religious ends as made possible within the
plentitude of God.  Heim emphasizes the Trinitarian tradition
in which God's self-revelation in Christ widens the scope of
God's grace and in which the coeternality of the Spirit, which
blows where the Spirit wills, makes relationships with peoples
of other faiths vital.  Furthermore, the Trinitarian focus on
communion, loving relationships, and Jesus' own self-giving
love requires interfaith dialogue and community seeking for
justice.[135]  Heim finds Knitter's emphasis on justice to be
valuable, linking religious reality to historical existence in
ways that other pluralists fail to do.[136]

Heim's critique of religious pluralism is incisive.  Nevertheless, his assertion of a plurality of religious goals not only
within history, but beyond death, is questionable.  One cannot question that the aims/goals of a religion mold present
experience, practice and thought.  The goal of the Theranda
Buddhist leads to endless hours of meditation seeking the
liberated self.  However, to move from the present to the other
side of death is highly questionable.  Heim's argument is
based on salvation as primarily an individual event and the
result of individual achievement.  It appears that the major
premise for this assertion is that if this were not true then "the
universe is organized neither in accord with principles of
equity we recognize nor with the processes of development we

conceive."[137]   Heim continually speaks of religious fulfillment as something to be achieved, and within this definition of "salvation" he argues for the necessity of equity and developmental process.

From my perspective, God's action within and fulfillment of life is not an achievement but an absolutely gracious, surprising gift.  It is a costly gift offered from God's love and God's freedom.  This costly gift, which is loose in the cosmos, is concretized in Jesus Christ crucified and raised.  As a radically surprising gift it need not recognize equity nor developmental process.  This is precisely the point of Jesus' parable of the laborers in the vineyard (Matt. 20:1-16), and Paul's understanding of justification by grace through faith. This is total divine love, which is poured out upon all creation and all humanity and which, in spite of our religious goals and achievements, will fulfill a transformed humanity with awesome joy transcending all heavens, paradises, and Nirvanas.[138]  Heim's model, although developed within a Christian theological world, has more in common with the Hindu understanding of karma, where for every action there is necessarily a reaction.  From Heim's perspective, one creates one's own future rather than receiving one's future as a gift.

Furthermore, Heim's presentation would seem to lead to the absurd conclusion that any life on the other side of death is compartmentalized into a heavenly mansion for Buddhists, another for Muslims, another for Hindus, another for Christians, etc. This polysalvationism would affirm that human visions rather than God's transforming grace will create the future of the universe. I would interpret the Jesus of the Gospel of John to say that "in my Father's house there are many rooms/mansions," therefore there will be room for all of you. Jesus is not saying "fear not, you will not be disturbed by members of different religious communities here"!

## Conclusion

This journey along the contemporary theological Rubicon has surveyed a number of theological models for understanding interfaith relationships.  My own reflections have appeared in portions of the journey and indicate that I may be located somewhere within the inclusivist camp.  Three major factors spelled out in the chapter place me there.

One, I am convinced that the Abba and Spirit of Jesus are identified and concretized in Jesus crucified and raised. Therefore one may simply trust that the costly, vulnerable, serving, all-embracing and transforming love that comes to expression in the Jesus of flesh and blood flows forth from the heart of God. We can trust that this is true for the whole cosmos, all humanity, and ourselves. Two, I am convinced that the Abba and Spirit of Jesus are universally loose in the world, and their presence and activity are within all creation and every people. We should never be surprised by the wondrous gift and consequences of that hope, that faith. Three, the heart and mind of the universe is one. "Hear O Israel, the Lord is one" (Deut. 6) and the destiny of all reality and of all humanity is one in God who raised Jesus from the dead and poured out God's Spirit for the sake of all creation!

## CHAPTER 4

# Proclaiming Crucified Truth:
## Dialogical Witness within Religious Pluralism

### Dialogical Witness within Religious Pluralism

We began this discussion by developing a 21st-century contextualized missiology of the cross. The discussion focused upon God's costly, transforming, all-embracing love concretized in Jesus' mission and cross. This is a missiology of the reign (kingdom) of God embodied in Jesus, marked by solidarity with pain, struggles for justice and the wholeness of life, limited to the power of a vulnerable love that persuades, perseveres, and culminates in a proclamation of the crucified and raised Truth. The discussion concluded with a call to allow this incredible vision of God's unconditional grace to transform our perspectives of religious pluralism.

We then surveyed contemporary models through which Christians understand their relationship to people of other faiths. In this chapter we ask specifically how and whether we can confess Jesus Christ within religious pluralism.

We have noted that it has been suggested that an abandonment of Christian claims to Jesus' uniqueness or normativeness would be a decisive step in moving humanity into a common future. It has also been argued that contemporary scholarship forces us to move in this direction because it will not allow any particular historical factor to be universalized, since all faith perspectives are culturally conditioned. Furthermore, it is asserted that religious claims to finality and normativeness always result in culturally oppressive and politically imperialistic mission practices.

I appreciate the concerns of those who critique the church's faith and mission from the perspective of cultural relativism and international cultural and political imperialism. However, the thesis of this book has moved in a different direction. This study asserts that it is a total acceptance of Jesus' uniqueness and Lordship by the Jesus movement that will enable the Christian community to make a creative contribution to the transformation of humanity and will also enable Christians to enter into genuine dialogue and community with peoples of other faiths. Only when the power of creative, life-transforming, persistent, persevering and vulnerable love, embodied in the crucified Jesus, becomes normative for the Christian community's proclamation and praxis will the church begin to be a transforming agent within the human community and a dialogical partner with the full human family. Only then will the Jesus movement authentically proclaim the life-transforming power of Christ as the crucified Truth.

## A Theology of the Cross as Prerequisite to Christian Witness within Religious Pluralism

### The Cross and God's Participation in Human Suffering

The resurrection faith proclaims that Jesus Crucified is the one who is raised from the dead, sits at the right hand of God, and the one to whom the future belongs. The resurrection announces that, contrary to human expectations, Christ's way of the cross is God's way in the world.[139] That means, among other things, that the suffering mission of Jesus Crucified manifests God's participation in the suffering of the broken human community.

Before other dimensions of a missiology of the cross are mentioned, it is necessary to note implications for mission already evident. In relation to all human suffering, the Christian faith asserts that God knows and shares the suffering experienced and inflicted upon the human family. "I have heard the cry of my people and know their suffering" (Exod. 3). All forms of suffering, including poverty and oppression, constantly raise questions concerning the absence, the silence, the judgment, or even the righteousness of God. In spite of all the signs that would indicate otherwise, the gospel of the crucified and risen Jesus proclaims that God loves so deeply that God is with us—Emmanuel—and suffers with us. That is in itself good news.

Jesus crucified calls the body of Christ to follow him into the depths of human suffering and pain. It is there that good news is to be announced and celebrated. The Abba of Jesus is not indifferent to the world, nor does God speak at a distance from the world but is personally present and passionately involved with the world. Those who witness to Jesus are likewise called by the crucified and risen Jesus Christ to witness among people and within pain. Any form of indifference among disciples and any attempt to communicate the gospel from a distance while avoiding participation in the pain and tragedy of human brokenness is a denial of Jesus' finality (normativeness) and a denial of authentic dialogical witness.

On January 19, 1992, Albert Glock, an ELCA missionary, was murdered near Birzeit University on the West Bank. Glock was a professor of archeology at Birzeit University. He had begun his career like most Western biblical archeologists, exploring the ancient civilizations of the Middle East. However, he became aware of the fact that there was little concern for the last 500 to 1,500 years when the land was inhabited by the Palestinian Arab peoples. He saw this history ignored as recent history was scraped away to plumb the culture of the ancient Middle East—the times of Abraham, Jeremiah, or the Maccabees. In that process, he saw one more attempt to deny a Palestinian people their own land, history and tradition. With that concern primary in his mind, he gave his life to enabling Palestinian people to discover through archeology their own place within the history of the nations. In particular, he documented Israel's destruction of two hundred Palestinian villages. I believe that it was this struggle that led to his execution. Glock and his wife, Lois, chose to be in solidarity with a suffering and exploited people, both Muslim and Christian. The suffering-with-us God had called Al and Lois to be participants in the suffering-with-us body of Christ. "If one member suffers, all suffer together" (I Cor. 12:26). All authentic dialogue and witness is and begins in solidarity with people in their joys and in their pain.

### The Cross of Jesus and the Divine/Demonic Struggle

Jesus was crucified because he challenged and contradicted the religious, social and ethical values and decisions of his contemporaries. Jesus stood within the tradition of Israel's prophets, proclaiming the arrival of that which they had envisioned, the kingdom of God (Luke 10:23), and calling Israel to repentance. He denounced many of Israel's religious elite as "blind guides," "whitewashed tombs," "hypocrites." In striking contrast to their lives and teaching, he called for forms of mercy, justice and righteousness that transcended their moral legalism, and he proclaimed a form of grace that shattered their religious structures. Jesus announced forgiveness for those who had been ostracized and damned, infuriating the religious establishment. He called for mercy and justice for the poor. He liberated the possessed and healed the sick. He denounced the temple priesthood for transforming God's house of prayer into a commercial venture. Jesus' life-transforming ministry contrasted strikingly with those who focused on tithing mint, dill and cumin (Matt. 23:23). Jesus' denunciation of religious hypocrisy, mercilessness, and social irresponsibility in the name of his Father (Abba) inflamed his enemies.

Jesus' prophetic struggle pitted the kingdom of God against the kingdom of evil (Luke 11). The kingdom of God was embodied in Jesus. The realm of darkness was embodied in priests, rabbis, throngs and Roman authorities who pushed Jesus out of the world and onto a cross. Destructive powers alive within historical agencies rejected Jesus' mission of mercy, justice and righteousness and nailed Jesus to the cross. In this struggle for mercy, justice and righteousness, God in Christ suffered in and for the world.

This exploration into a missiology of the cross places God within a historical, prophetic struggle for righteousness and justice. Jesus Christ, nailed to a cross, as prophet of God, proves beyond any shadow of doubt that God has a passionate concern for transforming the lives of those who are ostracized, damned, demon-possessed, poor, oppressed or sick. That is good news! The transformation of life in the name of God and the suffering servant Jesus is at the heart of the *Missio Dei* and something worth living and dying for.

Braaten writes in *The Apostolic Imperative*:

The cross has all too often been cloistered within the

Sunday piety of the church, rather than being the dynamic of the everyday soldiers of the cross fighting for justice within the economic, social and political situations of life.

Although there are other humanitarian groups at work to alleviate suffering and degradation, poverty and hunger, the church will want to be second to none in doing everything within its power to lift the burdens of the millions who starve, the races that are humiliated, the nations that are held captive, and the classes that are deprived of full equality, etc.[140]

The mission of the body of Christ is determined by its head and Lord who is normative for the vision of the *Missio Dei*. Any mission carried out in Jesus' name is compelled to participate in the kingdom's struggle for mercy, justice and righteousness—for the transformation of life. Dialogical witness must take place within God's transforming movement within life.

### The Cross of Jesus and the Church's Vulnerability in Mission

The church that proclaims repentance and forgiveness in Jesus' name (Luke 24:47) is called to walk the same path as its Lord and Master. In contrast to human inclinations, God-like and Christ-like forgiveness rather than retaliation is to be a mark of the church. Furthermore, in contrast to those who rule the Gentiles, Jesus says to those who follow him as disciples, "Whoever would be first among you must be slave of all" (Mark 10:44). These normative mandates of Jesus condemn all attempts by Christians to witness from the perspective of cultural or societal power. It calls us to share the mission of the body of Christ, molded by the mind of Christ (Phil. 2:5-11) who, half naked, washed his disciples' feet. All contemporary critiques of our Christian arrogance and imperialism were previously and powerfully made by the Lord of the church.

Only as the church takes the biblical finality and normativeness of the cross seriously can it authentically witness to the uniqueness of Jesus Christ as Lord within religious pluralism. The body of Christ has the privilege of witnessing to a seemingly incredible vision of God in Jesus Crucified. In Jesus, God shares the depths of our pain and participates in the struggle for life and justice. Contrary to human expectation, God incredibly appears as the crucified, redeeming slave of the universe standing in solidarity with victims and offering forgiveness to victimizers. The crucified Jesus with nail-pierced hands and wounded side sits at the right hand of God and is normative for the *Missio Dei.*

Participation in the messianic mission of God that actualizes God's future must be conformed to this cruciform, vulnerable, self-giving love manifest in Jesus the Cosmic Crucified. "As the Father has sent me, so I send you" (John 20:19-23). Wesley Ariarajah, former Director of the World Council of Churches' interfaith studies program, asserts that religious pluralism demands that Christian witness be given in the spirit of one who has truly experienced the humility, the vulnerability and the self-giving that are at the center of Christ's own witness.[141] Our study of the biblical faith affirms that Jesus Crucified mandates that there is no other way in which any witness to God's Truth may authentically be given.

The announcement of this incredible vision of the kingdom of God incarnate in Jesus Crucified is to be carried by a people who are empowered by the vision and called to walk as humble participants within the vision. When the church in trust follows Jesus into the depths of human pain, when it participates in the struggle for universal justice and is molded by the crucified mind of Christ, granting forgiveness even to the enemy, then it witnesses authentically to Jesus. Then the church begins to witness to that One who transcends cultural relativism and who is the norm for all the manifestations of the Holy within the cosmos.

If we are not prepared to take this crucified Jesus as absolute Lord of our own lives and the life of the church, if this missiology of the cross does not provide the core of our faith and mission, we should replace our talk about the uniqueness and normativeness of Jesus with an honest Christian cultural relativism.

## Dialogical Witness within Religious Pluralism

### Religious Relativism and God's Universal Presence

As noted in Chapter 3, religious relativists, including Christian scholars, assume the universality of the presence of God or "The Holy," the activity of a cosmic saving power, a multiplicity of revelatory events, and the absence of any normative revelation by which all revelatory claims may be critiqued. Within the context of Christian history, often marked by intolerance and cultural imperialism, one may hear the gospel of universal relativity as a breath of fresh air that might impede the religious fanaticism which has been experienced in Bosnia, Kosovo, Lebanon, Northern Ireland, American fundamentalism, and the present American self-righteous and arrogant imperialism as well as the more sophisticated forms of Christian intolerance present in the church's documents and institutions.

There are very attractive aspects to the relativist approach to religious truth. God is recognized as universally present to the whole of creation. Furthermore, the whole human family has the potential for imaging God. The following emphases are recognized as major biblical themes: God's creation of and presence within every corner of the cosmos (Gen. 1, Ps. 139); God's universal pervading wisdom within humanity (Prov. 8, Rom. 2); God's planting of the human search for God within the heart of all peoples (Acts 17); and God's intention to reconcile the whole of creation (Eph. 1:9-10). These themes are made concrete in Melchizedek (Gen. 14), Jethro (Exod. 18), and many others. Furthermore, as we noted in Chapter 1, such emphases are supported by Jesus' own message and mission, the New Testament witness, and Christian experience that continually encounters persons of integrity and openness to God's will outside the Christian tradition. Christians rooted in creation as God's gift are always called to listen for the love and will of God in human voices of every religious family and to look for the imprints of God's presence in every culture.

### Dialogical Witness: Mutual Listening-Affirmation, Understanding and Enrichment

Dialogical witness is first of all participation in God's self-giving and vulnerable love for people. Divine love always includes concern for the value and well-being of the one loved and necessarily affirms the other. Love affirms people, creating somebodies out of nobodies.

One of the most powerful ways that love affirms people is by listening to them. Listening to them values and respects their inner life and being. Vulnerable love goes further and through listening is willing to receive and value the inner life of the other, even though it may sound strange or dissonant. Dialogical witness in participation with Jesus Crucified, necessitates listening love as affirmation and respect of someone created in the image of God and who is embraced by the suffering love of God.

The three great missionary communities—Islam, Christianity and Buddhism—as well as other religious traditions call for and desire mutual witness. Mutual witness can take place only if Buddhists, Muslims and Christians for example actually understand each other. Authentic Christian witness among Buddhists depends on Buddhists' actually hearing the biblical witness to Jesus. Authentic Muslim and Buddhist witness among Christians depends on Christians' actually hearing the messages of Muhammad and the Buddha. In order to understand another person's faith and effectively witness to Jesus Crucified, it is essential to understand the faith of Muslims and Buddhists as they believe it to be understood.

There are innumerable barriers to this sharing of faith and insights through witness. The centuries of separation and alienation demand that the Christian community take the cruciform mission of the church within the Muslim and Buddhist worlds seriously. Furthermore, the centuries of religious and theological misunderstanding demand that patient in-depth dialogue always be the context for witness to the faith.

Because persons of faith and rich religious traditions are found within Christian, Jewish, Muslim, Buddhist and other communities, sincere and honest dialogue cannot be anything other than enriching. In his book *Beyond Dialog*, John B. Cobb Jr. states that dialogue between Buddhists and Christians has possibilities for mutual enrichment and what he calls mutual transformation as dialogue enables all participants to see their own vision from new and valuable perspectives.[142]

## Within an Age of Relativism
## Proclaiming the Normative Crucified Jesus

The biblical faith challenges us to move from religious relativism to Jesus as normative: Jesus proclaimed as Messiah (Luke 24), heavenly Lord (Phil. 2:5-11), cosmic judge (Matt. 25), universal reconciler (Eph. 1:9-10), that one in whom the fullness of God was pleased to dwell (Col. 2:9-10). One can choose to reject this claim to transcendence of relativity as itself a relative cultural form that must be eliminated for the sake of the future of humanity. I am convinced otherwise. Authentic discipleship of Jesus will lead Christians beyond an enlightened relativism to a deep, Christ-like concern for and involvement in human lives for the sake of universal peace and justice. Christians are called beyond mutual respect grounded in God's universal creative presence to a vulnerable love grounded in Christ's love that embraces even those who consume God's creation and children. Jesus' radical call to love of the enemy, rooted in God's embrace of both the children of God and the enemies of God, is the hope of the human family.

In the world of postmodernism, I am convinced that Jesus in life-transforming, persistent, vulnerable and all-embracing love transcends cultural relativity. There are reasons within faith that indicate that Jesus' finality is Truth for all life in all times and all places. *Behind our relative historical, cultural experiences of life which are so varied is an awareness that love, caring, community and belonging are essential for all of life. Caring community transcends cultural relativity.* Furthermore, there is an inner witness that persuades us that the love and compassion embodied in Jesus is of ultimate value for life, making a claim upon our lives. There is also an inner testimony that persuades us that the community-bonding love embodied in Jesus is of God (Col. 2:9-10) and that the compelling voice in scripture that witnesses to this Truth is the voice of the Spirit of God. Furthermore, the gospel proclaims a vision of God that if not true should be true. Nowhere else is the ultimate Mystery of the universe described as so deeply and passionately involved in human brokenness for the sake of human life. It may be argued that this vision of God is merely the figment of the human imagination, but I believe that no one can deny that it is a vision unsurpassable in depth and breadth. In the words of Anselm, it is that than which nothing greater can be conceived.[143] The resurrection, experienced by the disciples as an empty tomb and living presence, is an external witness that, in concert with inner convictions and the inner voice of the Spirit, proclaims that Jesus Crucified is raised and sitting at the right hand of God, transcending historical relativity, and is normative for life. There is no inherent reason for saying that is impossible. It is true that historiography assumes that historical evidence must be verifiable by the criteria of historiography; however, there is no logically necessary reason for denying that the nonverifiable has occurred.

This evidential argument of faith is not logically necessary (a theology of the cross assumes that), but neither is it logically impossible or irrelevant for the 21st century. If our skepticism leaves us with nothing but a wager on eternity, I, for one, wish to wager on Jesus Crucified. If doubt says it may not be true, I prefer to live with those doubts, sharing a possible unsurpassable vision with Jesus and his people, than to share with certainty something less than can be conceived (Anselm) or dreamed. If, however, by the witness of the Holy Spirit we actually come to believe that the gospel is true, then the Christian community possesses a hidden treasure that is so incredible and of such wonderful import that we will find it impossible to cease from witnessing to God's grace revealed and given in Jesus Christ for the sake of the universe.[144]

### God, Jesus, and Our Hope
### for the Transformation of All Reality

God—the whence of all reality, the permeating life and order of the universe—is concretized in Jesus. It is important to emphasize that the New Testament, as noted above, sees that Incarnation as unique, normative and unsurpassable. God is universally present, revealed and experienced. However, faith trusts that because Jesus concretizes the Heart of the universe, the revelation in Jesus also norms all revelation and all religious experience. God is none other and will not be other than God revealed in Jesus, and therefore the Cosmic Vulnerable Companion willing to share human agony as suffering servant in order that the cosmos might move from darkness into light. As a Christian, I trust that no present or future revelation may contradict or supersede that assertion. From this perspective, salvation as forgiveness, the transformation of life and hope is rooted in this God incarnate in Jesus. The present and the eternal future of every person within the cosmic family and the ultimate re-creation and reconciliation of the universe are totally dependent upon the God concretized in Jesus. There is no other God than the one embodied and decisively identified at Golgotha.

This celebration of the normative revelation and saving event embodied in Jesus is not to be mistaken for the assertion that the present transformation and the eternal destiny of every person depends upon meeting this Jesus through the preaching of the gospel within history or being recognized members of our Christian institutions.

John writes that to meet Jesus Crucified is to confront judgment and life:

> For God sent the Son into the world, not to condemn the world, but that the world might be saved through him. [The one] who believes is not condemned, [the one] who does not believe is condemned already.... This is the judgment, that the light has come into the world and [people] loved darkness rather than light, because their deeds were evil. (John 3:16-21)

This passage affirms that a positive or negative response to Jesus is a response to the Word of God, which pours forth from the Heart of the galaxies. The passage, similar to other biblical texts (Acts 4:12), makes assertions about those who have had the privilege of meeting Jesus. Those who have met Jesus and trusted in the vulnerable, creative love embodied in Jesus have already passed from darkness into light, from death to life. They already dwell within the incredible reality of God's Truth incarnate in Jesus, the magnificence of the messianic reign of God in Christ. In the words of Rom. 10:13-17, they have called upon the name of the Lord and have been saved.

The Johannine passage just quoted and similar texts also indicate that those who have met Jesus and rejected God's truth made flesh and blood in Jesus have already been judged as outside the messianic kingdom, "because they loved the darkness rather than the light." These texts do not make any statement about those who have not met the Truth or seen the Light in Jesus, who have not yet encountered the incredible love that pours out of the Heart of galaxies embodied in Jesus. There are multitudes who have never met the Truth and Light of Jesus even through they have heard of Jesus and listened to the story of Jesus. We as Christians have often so distorted Jesus Crucified that we have made it impossible for Grace and Truth (John 1:14) in Jesus to be known. Our distortion of life and our mangled theological attempts at witness to the Truth have hidden and distorted the Crucified Truth concretized in the cross of Jesus. Centuries of Christian contempt for the Jewish community as well as centuries of Christendom's imperialism would certainly exemplify and verify this.

Questions are often raised by evangelical Christians as to how God relates with those who have never encountered the Truth concretized in Jesus. Faith may trust that God embraces the total universe with the same compassion, grace, forgiveness and acceptance that is concretized in Jesus and offered to us. Their relationship to the Heart of the universe, as ours, is grounded in the pain and suffering love of God embodied and revealed in Jesus, although their call to repentance and Truth may come through other voices. We trust that the Abba and Spirit of Jesus are loose in the universe, and that means that Spirit-created signs and visions are possible anywhere and everywhere. The saving power of the Abba and Spirit of the universe are present and active within every person and culture, accepting, calling, and drawing all humanity into the fullness of life and community.

## Mission, Dialogue and Witness: Conclusion

As disciples of the crucified Jesus, we are sent into the world with a treasure that is beyond human comprehension. We believe that this treasure is an unfathomable gift within the human community and is to be shared with the universe. However, we share it as persons who know that God has preceded our witness, that we will meet people from other faiths who may surpass us in insights into truth and even insights into the gospel, as well as in moral and religious integrity. We will also share that treasure as disciples called to share with the crucified Lord the human suffering and struggle for life and justice. Finally, we will share the gospel treasure as persons called to an openness and vulnerability embodied in Jesus. That means listening and receiving in order that we may begin to understand, love, and know other persons who are created in the image of God who goes and continues to go through hell on their behalf. We are called in our mission, witness and dialogue to embody with Christ a gentle, patient strength in listening and witness. "A dimly burning wick [the servant] will not quench" (Isa. 42:3). Both dialogue and witness will take the form of half-naked servants at the world's feet.

**CHAPTER 5**

# In the Name of Jesus Crucified:
### Engaging Global Injustice
### with Global Faith-Communities

## Introduction

The Winter Olympics in Nagano, Japan, opened with a colorful ceremony. Representatives of the global community who gathered to participate in the winter games marched into the arena clothed in the styles of a multitude of countries. Three billion members of the human family watched via television as the citizens of Japan welcomed us to their homeland in the mountain country north of Tokyo through moving cultural symbols. I was mesmerized by the gigantic choir led by the Japanese conductor, who is employed halfway around the world as the director of the Boston Symphony Orchestra. Powerfully, the choir sang "Ode to Joy" with its references to the one human family. Then, through the miracle of modern fiberoptic technology, the choir in Nagano was joined with choirs from Sydney, Australia; Cape Town, South Africa; London, England; and the United Nations building in New York City.

This event manifests what is being identified as globalization, one global village, created as modern technology compresses time and space. This is the context of mission and service today in the 21st century. Robert Schreiter in his book *The New Catholicity* lists a number of features of this contemporary globalization process, including that the world is dominated by one political and national power, the United

States, since the collapse of the Soviet Union; that capitalism and the free market dominate the economic global landscape; and that instantaneous electronic communication increasingly weaves the global community into one vast network of relationships.[145]

## Mission Voices from the Center of Power

Significant consequences for the life and mission of the church have been the result of globalization. Obviously, the phenomenon has been emerging over hundreds of years. That process has led to a point where we in the United States are at the center of world power. Furthermore, we are at the center of power precisely when the compression of time and space is accelerating at a breathless pace. This reality comes to expression in many ways. The simple fact that we as Americans can travel almost anywhere in the world and speak and be understood in English illustrates this phenomenon.

I awoke at 1:30 a.m.. one morning to watch by television Kofi Annan and Tariq Aziz being questioned by reporters from around the world. The news conference, held in Baghdad, Iraq, was being conducted in English, the international language of contemporary globalization. Reporters from China-TV, Jordanian newspapers and a host of others asked questions in English. Annan and Aziz responded in English. That phenomenon was made possible by hundreds of years of globalization. Science and technology produced machines that resulted in the British Industrial Revolution. That revolution produced a gigantic economic and military machine, which developed communication and transportation systems and resulted in the British Empire. The English language began to encircle the globe. The Second World War, made possible by innovations in military hardware and communications, ended with a British-American victory. At the end of the war the United States was producing and consuming one-half of the world's total wealth. This economic and military power has led to American domination within the world community.

Can a church living and working within the center of global power authentically participate in the mission of the body of Christ? History forces us to ask this question, because past Christian communities living at the center of world power have failed. The original documents of the Christian community were written in Greek. Greek was the international language of the day, a fact made possible by the victories of Alexander the Great who conquered the then-known world. The early church moved out of a small, marginal, Aramaic-speaking Jewish community into the Roman Empire. For over two centuries it was a marginal community whose members witnessed in the Greek language to their faith in Jesus Christ. They were often persecuted by the established powers for challenging in the name of Jesus the values and customs of the day. However, in the fourth century the Emperor Constantine accepted the Christian faith, and Christianity became the religion of the State. It was then, through the Greek language of the Byzantine Empire, that Christian orthodoxy was imposed on the inhabitants of the Empire. Christians now persecuted "heretics" and "pagans" for their lack of conformity to the new Christian society.

The official language of the Western church was Latin. Originally, Latin was the international language of the Roman Empire and its legions of soldiers. The early church permeated the Roman world as a community of the marginalized, suffering through two centuries of persecution. When the church began to emerge as a major voice in the West, the military and political power of Rome was collapsing. The church became a power in this political vacuum. Later the Latin church, in cooperation with European ethnic groups and kings, developed into the Holy Roman Empire. The Holy Roman Empire, often with the threat of death, imposed Latin Christianity on the rest of Europe. In the years following 1492, the "Christian" royalty of Portugal and Spain "cleansed" the Iberian peninsula of Muslims and Jews. They then set sail for America, as well as portions of Africa and Asia, in order to conquer the world for Spain, Portugal, the Pope and Jesus Christ. The brutal destruction of people and cultures is a matter of record. Again I ask, is it possible for a Christian community at the center of world power to authentically participate in the mission of the body of Christ? If the "sacred" languages of marginalized Christian communities, Greek and Latin, were transformed into the language of Christendom's oppression, has it not also happened to the language of English as it became the medium through which the gospel is proclaimed among the nations?

The history of Western imperialism is the history of the intertwining of the Christian witness with the power of Western expansion. Within the context of this discussion of the mission of the global church, it is necessary to remind ourselves that Western expansionism has always been explosively fueled by white racism, which views nonwhite people and their cultures as inferior or uncivilized. There have always been prophetic voices crying out against this unholy alliance of religion and state, and there have always been Christian witnesses who have been molded by the mind of Christ. However, more often than not, the Christian witness that moved out of the centers of English-speaking power have been twisted and distorted by racism, cultural prejudices and societal values, thus betraying the original witness of the New Testament to Jesus, the crucified Messiah. In his book *Missionary Conquest*, George Tinker documents the inability of missionaries witnessing among the Native American nations to separate the witness of the gospel from their cultural values and customs. Tinker notes that John Eliot, the 17th-century missionary to New England, actually wrote that it was first necessary to move native peoples out of their traditional surroundings and into "civilized" towns before they could be prepared for baptism.[146] Evangelical enthusiasts may perceive this warning about unholy alliances as a sign that there are those within the church who have simply lost their missionary nerve. They would say that we must simply accept the fact that the church is paradoxically made up of sinners and saints. This is always a fact, so let us get on with the job!

Recently I was once again reminded of the horrifying consequences of "just getting on with the task." Marc Ellis, author of *Unholy Alliance*, is a powerful prophetic voice who speaks from his own isolation within the Jewish community.[147] In addressing a group of Christians at the Lutheran School of Theology at Chicago, he described what he sees as the great tragedy of his own people. The Jewish people, from his perspective, have moved from being a marginalized community within Western culture to a major player in world power politics. They also have moved from the indescribable suffering of fiery furnaces, where millions of Jewish people were slaughtered in the attempt to rid the Aryan race of their presence, to a "Constantinian" people who now are in the process of oppressing and destroying a Palestinian people. Ellis concluded with a reminder that the Christian community shares the same kind of history and guilt. He noted that we live after 1492, after the imperialistic conquest, after slavery, after Auschwitz, after Bosnia, after Rwanda, after Kosovo, after Iraq, after _____, fill in the blank.

A number of years ago, Kosuke Koyama told a few of us who were working on a mission statement that any plans for mission that were to move out from the center of Western power into Asia had to begin with a recognition of the horrors of the past and deep repentance. Within a Christian context, repentance always means a reversal of direction, a move from our road to God's road, from participation in the norms and values of contemporary culture to participation in the mission of God embodied in Jesus, the crucified Christ. That means being called by God into conformity with the humble and vulnerable servanthood of Jesus. It means listening to Jesus say, "Take up your cross and follow me." We are called into this reality of the marginalized, prophetic mission of God that flows from the Holy Spirit's witness to Jesus Christ. We must live and think in repentance, and in faith in the God of Jesus. As citizens of the U.S., we must continually ask to what extent the U.S. Christian churches are one more manifestation of a church within the center of global power attempting to speak of truth which has often been distorted by the cultural context that insidiously permeates our lives.

The church at the margins of the power structures may rightfully ask us, "How can a church located within a culture where the mission outreach of the Christian community seems to be withering on the vine speak to the church whose evangelical outreach seems to be exploding?" Or how can a church saturated with the materialistic values of global capitalism speak to the world about the Holy Spirit, deep spirituality, human dignity, justice and sacrificial service? Or, as a conference at the University of Chicago heard from James Cone several years ago, how can a church divided on Sunday morning by racism witness authentically to Jesus? Or how can a church deeply entrenched in Western culture recognize the values and possibilities of contextualization in another culture? This is not to say that U.S. churches cannot say something significant. Jesus himself said that even the rich can be saved through the miraculous activity of God. Even a missionary community marked by Western imperialism and systemic racism can be used by God to bring forth fruits—where once again the body of Christ is alive among the marginalized peoples of Asia, Africa, and Latin America.

However, our eyes and ears here must be open to voices from these margins of the power structures where God's truth in Christ is more apt to be manifest than among us. Perhaps the most important point that we can make is that the most authentic voices of the mission of Christ may be found elsewhere, hidden on the continents of Africa, Latin America and Asia or within the marginal communities of the United States and Europe.

## Mission Out of the Capitalistic World

The collapse of the Soviet Union marked the end of the socialist-communist experiment, which no longer competes with global capitalism for global influence. This major event at the end of the 20th century has had devastating economic consequences for the marginalized people of the world, who have been even further marginalized.

Capitalism and the free market dominate the world. The development of instantaneous global financial transactions has led to a global economic system that has created a unified and interdependent global market. Global stock markets operate twenty-four hours a day, and massive amounts of capital move from continent to continent in micro-seconds (over one trillion dollars a day), threatening the financial stability of the most powerful countries. The collapse of the Thai *bat* or the Indonesian *rupiya* threatens the world market. International capitalistic institutions rush to infuse capital funds into threatened countries in order to prevent an international financial meltdown. Countries that are active players in this capitalistic system reap the benefits of being consumers and producers for the world market. Those that cannot compete in selling and buying, for example, Africa, are relegated to the "scrap heap" of the international system. Senator Paul Simon, speaking to the ELCA bishops at an annual educational event, spoke of the extreme difficulty in moving Congress toward creative engagement on the African continent. Before leaving with President Clinton on a trip to Africa, Commerce Secretary William Daley said, "Basically, Africa is a continent that has been left out of this century."

African theologian John Pobee writes, "Africa is not on the map because it does not seem to be a profitable market. Millions of youth and women are not on the map. Suffering today takes the dramatic form of exclusions. Exclusion is the ultimate expression of the death of the poor."[148]

A powerful symbol of this global marginalization is found in Georgetown, the capital of the tiny country of Guyana on the northern coast of South America. In this small country with a population of 600,000 there are two huge embassies representing the United States and what was formerly the Soviet Union. This tiny nation was once the focus of international competition between communism and capitalism that resulted in financial aid coming into the country from two giant sources. With the disintegration of the USSR, not just one source of outside revenue and expertise disappeared but two, because world capitalism no longer had any interest in investing in a world where profits, if any, were minimal. Like many countries of Latin America and most of the continent of Africa, Guyana was written off by the West as an unprofitable region of the globe. Marginalized nations marked by extreme poverty are falling into even deeper poverty.

Peri Rasolandraibi, Director of the Mission and Development of the Lutheran World Federation, has spoken of the "backward countries of Africa." He speaks this way not because he sees the African continent as inferior, but because within the international capitalistic system they are powerless and their economies are in reality moving backward. Their international debts, often accumulated by irresponsible military regimes borrowing from irresponsible banks from the North, are bleeding African nations to death.

The gap between rich and poor, always manifest in some manner within human society, is now clearly growing within the global community. For example, the financial income of the top 1 percent of people in the world is equivalent to that of the lower 57 percent. According to the World Health Organization (WHO) there are 840 million hungry persons in the world whose caloric intake is not sufficient to enable them to develop to their full potential as human beings. Many of them suffer incredible physical and psychological consequences simply because they do not have sufficient food to eat. Thirty thousand children under the age of five die every day because of inadequate diets and the lack of primary health care! That is the equivalent of one hundred Boeing 747s crashing daily, each with three hundred children on board. That daily tragedy does not even register on the horizon of our consciousness. Again, the WHO notes that in many third-world countries, maternal mortality is the leading cause of death of women. There are 20 million refugees in the world who are separated from their homes by human violence or natural disaster. Thirteen million orphans on the continent of Africa have lost their parents to AIDS. Most of this human disaster takes place outside the United States and Western Europe. That is accounted for by the fact that the U.S., Europe and Japan make up 30 percent of the world's population but produce and consume 85 percent of the world's wealth. The U.S., with 4 percent of the world's population, has 20-25 percent of the world's wealth. But even in the U.S. there is a growing gap between the rich and poor. It is estimated that one out of five children in the U.S. is malnourished.[149]

## Mission Voices from the Marginalized

One of the miracles of the 20th century is the fact that the Christian community began growing at an incredible rate in those regions of the world where poverty was greatest. In 1900, 87 percent of the world's Christian population lived in Europe and the U.S. One hundred years later, 60 percent of the Christian world lives in Latin America, Africa and Asia. In 1900 there were thee to ten million Christians on the continent of Africa. Today it is estimated that that number is over 350 million. These Christian communities live in the midst of poverty and oppression. Living within this context of marginalization, they read the Bible with different eyes or from different perspectives. Passages that have been skipped over by Christians who live within established churches at the center of world power leap off the page for those who read them with empty stomachs or from within prison walls. This reading of the scriptures has resulted in another miracle that encircled the globe, a theological miracle emphasizing God's solidarity with the oppressed called liberation theology, Dalit theology, Black theology, and feminist theology. German theologian Michael Welker asserts, "Every credible act of asking about God and talking about God must confront the challenges and impetuses of these theologies."[150]

People living in poverty discovered that the God of the scriptures and the Father of Jesus is passionately concerned for the poor and the oppressed. In the prophets like Hosea, Amos, and Isaiah as well as in the Law and the Psalms, there was and is a call from God for justice for the poor and the oppressed. Amos shouted that God was not concerned about religious ceremonies and sacrificial rites but called for justice: "Let justice roll down like waters and righteousness like an ever-flowing stream" (Amos 45:24). Isaiah stated that God was not concerned about penance as sitting in sack-cloth and ashes, but God wanted a revolution in our lives: God wanted the hungry fed and the naked clothed (Isa. 58:6-7). Jesus himself said that the final judgment before the Son of Man would reveal that compassionate concern for the hungry, thirsty, lonely and naked is the most significant factor in life. Furthermore, the Son of Man is so focused upon the suffering ones that the Lord of the universe is passionately involved in their lives and divine reality shares the pain and the suffering of the least, the most marginalized within the human community. "Inasmuch as you did it to one of the least of these my sisters and brothers you did it to me" (Matt. 25:40). This biblical priority for compassion and justice strikes a resonating chord in the hearts of the oppressed. In many cultures poverty, illness and violent oppression have been signs of God's absence or even God's judgment. This was certainly true in Jesus' own day (e.g. Luke 13:1-5, John 9:2). It is precisely for this reason that Jesus told the parable of the rich man and Lazarus (Luke 16:19ff). Poverty was not a sign of the absence or judgment of God. It is why Jesus cried out, "Blessed are you poor, for yours is the reign of God" (Luke 6:20). In contemporary terms, the poor and the oppressed are a top priority for God. They are not forgotten, and they are not damned! They have a future with God. They too have been created in the image of God and have gifts and potential that neither they nor their oppressors have dreamed of (Acts 2:17-18).

In many non-Western cultures, the biblical message that God's saving activity includes the whole person and the whole community also strikes a sympathetic chord. This is true because these cultures, in contrast to the West, have never separated the human person into a spiritually oriented soul and a physical body. These cultures have assumed that humans are psychosomatic beings. They presuppose that God will address the whole person. In 1972, the Mekane Yesus Church of Ethiopia developed a document that was addressed to the Western churches. That church was disturbed by the fact that there were more financial resources available for relief and development than for evangelism. Many government funds were flowing out of Europe for relief and development that could not be used for evangelistic purposes. They could not understand how one could divide God's work into two compartments. How could one serve the body and not the spiritual life of the human family? How could one serve the spiritual life of the human family and not their physical needs? It is noteworthy that in recent years this Ethiopian church, which has one of the strongest relief and development programs of any church, has grown in membership at double-digit percentage numbers. At the present time, with a membership of over 3.3 million, it is strengthening its evangelism and leadership programs as more people are being trained to teach those who desire to be baptized.

## Mission Visioning from the Center of Power

What can Christians from the West learn and say in this global context? A few years ago, an ELCA staff person was visiting Africa for the first time. She was traveling with a small group of people through Zimbabwe during the time of a severe drought. They saw hundreds of malnourished and starving children along the way. They saw the elderly sleeping away to death under the dust-ridden trees of the countryside. Toward evening, entering Bulawayo and driving to their hotel, she saw the unbelievable sight of a green golf course with all the sprinklers on! That horrifying picture speaks volumes concerning the gap between the rich and the poor. It also is a parable of global life. It says to most of us in a world of stark contrasts that we live on the global country club and the sprinklers are on! What does it mean to live and view life from this perspective?

First, it means that we have a very limited perspective. If we are to catch a glimpse of God's perspective we must depend upon those who live elsewhere for glimpses of the whole. The global community has powerfully called to our attention that the whole includes millions of the dispossessed. They have pointed to the Bible, the source of our faith, which proclaims that the dispossessed are a priority for God. Jesus' own ministry focused there. The sick were healed, the blind saw, the lame walked, the lepers were cleansed, the demon-possessed liberated, the poor were promised the reign of God, the hungry were fed and promised that they would rejoice in being filled, and sinners and the morally marginalized were placed center stage at Jesus' dining table. The third-world perspective declares to the churches of the West, Take note! Christian mission that does not prioritize the poor and is not holistic is not the mission of the body of Christ. Christian mission that envisions its task from the global country club must focus on its responsibility and its answerability to the God of the dispossessed. It cannot say, with Peter, that we do not have silver and gold (Acts 43:6). It will have to answer to God who asks, "Where is your sister and brother?" (Gen. 4:9)

I would suggest that it may be only by the grace of God that we are allowed to participate in this dimension of the mission of the reign of God. Contemporary church history would indicate that when one analyzes the global church for the gifts to be found, the Western church does not stand out as having an abundance of gifts in the realm of evangelism, prayer, spiritual healing, or cultural sensitivity. Many, even within the Western church, recognize that our future as communities of faith may depend upon our openness to receive the gifts of the Spirit from our global companions. Even though we cannot claim to be rich in the gifts of the Spirit—faith, love and hope—living on the country club we have tremendous resources that could be used to address the problems of global hunger, suffering, oppression and injustice. The churches of America have access to vast financial, technological and organizational resources that can be dedicated to the mission of the body of Christ. However, they must be channeled in the Spirit of the crucified, suffering servant who washed his disciples' feet. This is not a simple task for a people who live within a community permeated with the spirit of competitive capitalism. It is almost impossible for a person within this culture to walk with persons of another culture without walking over them or in front of them. Once again, we live within the promise of Jesus that even the rich can be saved by a miracle of God. Even the members of the global country club, through the power of the Spirit, can accompany the churches of Africa, Latin America and Asia in mission. Within the global Christian community they can participate in the holistic mission of the body of Christ.

Within this promise of Christ is our assurance of the possibility of authenticity in mission, I believe that prophetic advocates of justice should suggest to Western churches that they immediately, as official policy, make concrete plans to double the amounts of money being channeled to programs of churches and Non-Governmental Organizations (NGOs) that address issues of health, poverty and oppression. Most of these programs make creative contributions to local communities as they emphasize self-reliance, development of local leadership, community organization, capacity building, and grassroots development in health, education, and agriculture. There is no need to create new development and relief programs, for there are hundreds of excellent programs available that simply need further funding. A 1998 UNICEF Report on the World's Children states that progress is being made in sub-Saharan Africa. The number of children dying before five years of age changed from one in five in 1960 to one in six in 1996. What is needed is a commitment of the church to increase funding and to make health and poverty issues as important as issues that deal with pastoral pensions, churchwide medical plans, ecumenical relationship statements, funding of colleges and seminaries, liturgical styles and numerous other items that receive primary attention within ecclesiastical discussion. This is not so much a suggestion to decrease funding for the programs mentioned as to prioritize the raising of new money out of our abundance. For example, within the ELCA, the bishops of the church could determine that hunger funds, will in the future, be 25 million dollars rather than 15. This would be a miraculous contribution to the Year of Jubilee theme, which many Christians celebrated at the end of the second millennium. Jesus said that the poor are God's first priority. A church that is not in conformity with this mission of God is out of touch with its master and teacher.

The churches also should recognize that one of the most effective ways of addressing health, poverty and justice issues is advocacy work at the local, county, state and national levels. There is need for increased funding and staffing at all of these levels. Several major international issues to be addressed relate to capitalism's dominant role around the globe—global debt and its consequences for the marginalized, international trade relationships and their negative effects upon less economically developed countries, and IMF-restructuring proposals without consideration for the most poor. These issues must be addressed from the perspective of both protecting the most vulnerable and seeking to equip marginal nations to participate in the global market system. Other global issues are: justice for the Palestinian people; human rights issues in the Sudan; racism; ethnic cleansing on all continents; natural and international disasters; health issues, particularly for women and children; and the exploitation of children in the workplaces and marketplaces around the globe.

Poverty issues also plague the United States. The growing gap between the rich and the poor in the U.S. is a great tragedy within the most powerful economy in the world. It is a national disgrace. The horrendous inequity between inner-city school funding and suburban educational funding in the U.S. is a primary example of this problem.[151] For example, in the state of Illinois, two thirds of the students are funded at $6,000 a year and one third of the students, most of whom live in suburban areas, are funded at $12,000 a year. A few years ago, the Governor's attempt to rectify this situation by moving from a property-tax–based educational system to a sales-tax system was defeated with much of the opposition coming from wealthy Chicago suburbs. The world and our nation are marked by innumerable forms of evil that create poverty, injustice and oppression. Within the U.S. context there is no more destructive power of evil than white racism contributing to the gap between rich and poor. The Christian community, corporately and individually, is called in this realm of dehumanization to speak up on behalf of life for the dispossessed.

As noted earlier, the church is 98.8 percent lay people who spend over 99 percent of their time in the world outside the walls of a sanctuary of corporate worship. In contrast to the clergy, whose primary call is normally to a ministry of word and sacrament, their call is to be light and salt in the secular arena. People are to be fed, the sick are to be healed, the children are to be cared for, youth are to be educated, families are to be housed, society is to function on behalf of the total community, the weak are to be protected, the violent and the greedy are to be opposed. Prophetic voices within the church must call their official spokespersons to lift up the calling of people to service in their daily lives.

The primary calling of lay persons is not to be lay assistants to the clergy in their word and sacrament ministries; rather, it is to see and experience their daily callings within their vocations and avocations in the world. I remember a deputy sheriff, who played lead guitar for a family choir, saying that one should not spend too much time in church when crime was rampant on the streets. Although this statement was made somewhat in jest, it is a profound truth. The church does not exist for itself. It is called by God for the sake of the world. The church's primary agents for transforming the world are those 98.8 percent of the community who live 99 percent of their lives outside "the holy gates" in service of their families, their communities and the world. The 21st-century church must ask this question: How are the 98.8 percent of the membership to be better equipped to serve the world, particularly the poor and dispossessed? One will probably hear the question of whether lay persons do not also have a calling to witness explicitly to their faith. I will mention an case in which a deputy sheriff has been seen praying with both rape victims and families who have had loved ones die in tradgic highway accidents.

In December 1985, I attended a conference on "Justification and Justice" in Mexico City. Before the conference began, local leaders took the participants on a geographically short but culturally long journey to see the garbage dumps outside that gigantic city. We were driven up a high hill from which we could look across a valley to see the burning waste that stretched over hills in the distance. I looked out over the valley and saw people moving within the wasteland—men, women and children. There were little shacks constructed within the fire and the smoke; families survived there by sifting through the garbage for things that could be sold in the market. What kind of inner strength did this take? As I stood as a distant country-club observer, something within me said that Jesus was not a fellow observer! Jesus was over there in the fire and the smoke. Jesus was looking through the garbage as a suffering participant. The cross is planted deeply in the garbage dumps of the world, and if we are to serve Jesus we need to take up our crosses and follow him into the pain and suffering of the world. We are to be present there to participate in God's messianic mission on behalf of life.

## Mission within One Vast Network of Global Relationships

The disciples of Jesus Christ are called into the life-transforming activity of the kingdom of God. The 21st-century context for that mission is marked by global religious pluralism. As members of the Western world, we were, until recently separated, from this religious diversity. Engagement with people of other faiths took place in Asia or Africa. Pluralism and diversity has always been a context of the life of the Christian communities upon "those" continents.

However, today as time and space are compressed, it is a reality for the whole global village. There are approximately 2.2 billion Christians around the world, 1.1 billion Muslims, 800 million Hindus, 350 million Buddhists, 100 million followers of Traditional Religions, 1 billion persons for whom the sacred is irrelevant and countless other smaller groups. The vast network of global relationships has made the world of religious pluralism a reality in our own time and space. In the city of Chicago alone there are 350,000 Muslims, 80,000 Hindus, 122,000 Buddhists and 220,000 Jews.[152]

It is essential to recognize that all attempts to address health, poverty and justice issues on a global scale must be done ecumenically and in dialogue with many faith communities. The biblical faith calls us to common visions and tasks on behalf of life.

This is not a new vision of relationships within religious pluralism; however, it often has been a hidden vision. It has biblical roots. First, the biblical tradition affirms that God is the creator of all reality, and that every human is created in the "image of God." (Gen. 1:27). This theological concept affirms that humanity has the potential for relationships with God and in some way has the possibility of imaging God and participating in the creative work of God. Proverbs 8 portrays God working with Wisdom at God's side. Proverbs then notes that when rulers judge righteously it is because wisdom is woven into the fabric of reality.

This faith perspective sees God present and at work throughout all creation and in every human being. Whenever a Muslim mother nurses her child and loves that child into life it is a manifestation that God's love and wisdom have been woven into creation. Whenever a Buddhist artist paints the beauty of nature, a secular engineer creates a life-sustaining structure, a Christian politician enacts legislation that will protect the weak from the greedy and the powerful, there the wisdom and grace of God are present in the fabric of creation. This means that even though God's intended plan for life is distorted by sin, it is still present in every human being and every culture, whether religious or secular. God's creative web of life is a global reality calling for common visions and efforts on behalf of life.

The gospel of Jesus Christ also calls us into that reality of life-affirming and life-transforming service. Speaking from the Lutheran tradition, the gospel proclaims that one is justified by grace through faith. One's relationship with God is sheer gift; therefore one is totally free to be about God's work in the world. One is freed from the impossible struggle of self-salvation and free to be a fellow servant of Christ in the suffering and pain of the world.

Earlier we noted that service for the marginalized as whole persons was at the center of Jesus' own servant ministry. When the early church, in its struggle with Gnosticism, proclaimed that the Father of Jesus created the world and that Jesus' mission was the incarnation of the mission of God, they were asserting that God, in love, intended life to bubble out of the desert of the flesh-and-blood world. The sick were to be healed, lepers cleansed, the lame walk, the blind see, and the marginalized placed center-stage. Creation was not to be devalued or denied but rather transformed! The future, whether this side of death or the far side, was to be a new creation. Miracle of miracles, sinners were to be forgiven, and those who fought to destroy the work of God were still loved and called to return to the Messiah's banquet in which the Master poured out his own life blood for the sins and the transformation of the world.

Such a vision of God's mission within religious pluralism compels the Christian community into relationships with people of other faiths. This God-intended engagement will mean experiences of friendship and mutual enrichment. However, that engagement must be centered in the possibility of the various communities' focusing upon the brokenness and the suffering of the human community. The question must be, How can we find common visions and tasks on behalf of life? World history is replete with examples of how religious plurality has resulted in death and destruction. We pray that the 21st century will be marked by visionary people who will recognize the life-enhancing possibilities of interfaith religious relationships and find within their own traditions values and directions that will make common visions and efforts on behalf of life possible. As Christians we pray that we might be grasped and empowered by the Abba and Spirit of Jesus.

*This essay is dedicated to Eva Leo,*
*a lay woman and artist, who knew and lived God, Jesus, compassion, and justice.*
*Good Friday, April 10, 1998.*

## CHAPTER 6

# Preaching Unfathomable Grace

## Sermon 1
### God of Galaxies in Flesh and Cross
Text: John 1:1-14

We gather under the theme "Witness within an Interfaith World." That is our reality today. Of the six billion people around the globe 2.2 billion are Christian (one-third), 1.1 billion are Muslim (one-fifth), 800 million are Hindu, 350 million are Buddhist. Closer to home, within the city of Chicago, for example, there are over 350,000 Muslims, 80,000 Hindus, 220,000 Buddhists, and 220,000 Jews. These are our surgeons, dentists, bankers, engineers. Even closer, they are our friends and may attend our services of worship.

Twenty-five years ago I was a pastor in Dubuque, Iowa. One day I visited a family that had moved into town and had visited our church. As I stepped into the living room I saw a large portrait of a prophetic figure. I asked who had painted this impressive portrait. The woman of the house said that she had painted it and that it was a painting of Maher Babba, a Guru who emerged out of India in the early 20th century. She told how a number of years ago she had gone through a difficult divorce while living in Louisiana. Her Christian friends had ostracized her, and she was depressed and lonely. She found acceptance and support from the local followers of Maher Babba.

How do we live and witness in this world where religious pluralism is increasingly a fact of life? During our worship and devotional experience we will focus upon two dimensions of our faith. One, we will listen to the scriptures to hear from the gospel of God's creative, all-embracing, healing, forgiving, suffering, vulnerable love, love that will never let us go! Nothing can separate us from that love that is made concrete, specific in the flesh and cross of Jesus. Second, we will listen to the scriptures to hear the proclamation of God that God's Word is alive, active and revealing within the totality of creation.

The Johannine text announces this gospel. In the beginning was the Word, the Wisdom, the Mind, the Heart—and this Wisdom, Word, Heart was with God and was God. Through this Wisdom all creation came into being. John says that this wisdom, logos, has always been at work, for this Mind/Word of God enlightens every person that comes into the world. It is this true light that makes it possible to say that humanity is created in the image of God. Then John says that this Wisdom, this Word, became flesh and tented/dwelt among us. No one has ever seen God, but this Word, dwelling intimately with God and now enfleshed, has made God known!

John begins the Gospel by announcing that that which one encounters in Jesus of Nazareth comes from the very Heart of the universe, the Heart and Mind of the center of galaxies. This is what is known in theology as a "high" Christology. John confesses a high Christology because he is convinced that the God encountered in Christ is the God who embraces all humanity, all creation, the whole universe.

John says that Jesus cannot be limited to being a Judean prophet; he cannot even be "the prophet" spoken of by Moses in Deuteronomy 18:18. Even John the Baptist exceeds that expectation. Furthermore, the Wisdom, Word of God encountered in Jesus, can't even be limited to a role as Messiah. Immediately in the first chapter of John, Philip finds Andrew and says, "We have found the one spoken of by Moses and the prophets, we have found the Messiah." We have found the one who fulfills the dreams of Isaiah when lions lie with lambs, children play with vipers, people sit under their own vines, and there is peace. Swords have been beaten into plows for cultivating the land. But this vision is not yet enough. It's still too provincial. It still often seems to center in a new temple, a new Jerusalem. That is too provincial for Jesus, for in speaking to the Samaritan woman, Jesus says that the hour is coming when true worshippers will not worship in Samaria nor in Jerusalem. They will worship in Spirit and truth. John will have nothing to do with "Temple Mount" theology (prevalent in the *Left Behind* series), nothing to do with building a temple or raising red heifers in Texas for future sacrifices. God, says John, is Spirit—Spirit active but hidden everywhere.

Furthermore, what one encounters in Jesus is not limited to the sons of Abraham, as some of Jesus' Johannine contemporaries were claiming. Jesus' high Christology is expressed in Jesus' words "before Abraham, I am." This is John's way of breaking out of religious exclusivism. God is not to be locked up in any box, even a new Jerusalem or Abraham-the-Father-of-three-religions box. What is encountered in Jesus bubbles forth from cosmic depths and comes from the source of all light and all life.

"And the Word became flesh and tabernacled among us." What does John tell us about that radical blinding revelation? I find it interesting that people of other religions intuitively see the wonder and uniqueness of the gospel while we have turned wonder into dead theologies that accelerate the heart of no one.

David Rahbar was a young Pakistani Qur'anic scholar who earned his doctorate at Cambridge University, England. As Rahbar worked with Christian friends he often heard the Christian critique of Islam: that Allah, the God of the Qur'an, is a capricious God; that one cannot know God or the trustworthiness of God; that God is a God of sheer power and will who predestines the masses of humanity to hell and saves an elect people for paradise. Rahbar rejected this critique, making a careful study of the Qur'an that resulted in a book, *The Justice of God.* Here argued that God is not capricious but can always be trusted to judge justly. One did not have to be terrorized by a hidden will of God; one could count on the justice of God. The straight path of God's will has been revealed, and resurrection and judgment are a future reality.

As Rahbar continued his studies, he talked to Christian friends, he read theology, and he read the Bible. Surprising everybody, one day he announced that he had been baptized. Muslim and Christian friends argued that it had been a rushed and rash decision. He wrote a letter describing his walk. Among other things, he said that in reading the New Testament he had been confronted with a perfect love. In the story of Jesus he had seen an all-encompassing love that not only embraced disciples and friends but even stretched out to enemies. Not only had Jesus said "love your enemies" (Matt. 5:43-48), he had forgiven those who drove spikes into his hands and feet. Jesus had said, "Father, forgive them, for they know not what they do."

Rahbar had concluded that this is perfect love, and only God is perfect, therefore Jesus must be from God. He said that he also had struggled in walking in perfect justice. He questioned whether he would be able to pass the test of a final judgment. He now found peace in the hands of unconditional grace.

This is the message of the New Testament. It is expressed in John's writing that Jesus is the Good Shepherd who lays down his life for his sheep. Even sheep who fail, deny and betray the Shepherd are loved, called, forgiven and sent. And John says it is this unconditional, serving, suffering, forgiving love that draws humanity to Jesus' cross. Jesus in John 12 says that in his death he will be glorified and that in his death, his being lifted up on the cross, he will draw the world unto himself.

John proclaims that out of the Heart of the universe, out of the Word, the Mind, the Wisdom of God, springs such compassion, which will gather and transform humanity and all creation. Faith trusts that this is true. This compassion pouring out like living water from the Heart of the universe is embodied in Jesus. This Word, particularized in the flesh and on the cross, holds galaxies and embraces all of life. It is true in your heart; it is also true billions and trillions of light years from here. It is true before any of us tells the story of Jesus— which is fortunate, because we will never get there. It is true when the sun ceases to shine and galaxies disintegrate. Jesus is the Way and the Truth and the Life, for in and through the Mind and Heart of God, made concrete in Jesus, one is allowed to enter the Holy of Holies of ultimate galactic mysteries.

I close with a glimpse from another Muslim, an artist. This story comes from Harold Vogelaar, who spent over twenty years in the Middle East and in Cairo. One day he met a young Egyptian artist who had just completed a portrait of a dashing Muslim swordsman holding a dove in one hand and a sword in the other. Harold asked about the symbolism in the picture. The artist replied that the dove meant that Islam always offered peace, but the sword meant that it was not always possible to offer peace. Islam had to defend itself; Mohammed as a statesman had to defend his community from Meccan merchants and armies. A sword became necessary. Furthermore, there was evil in the world that threatened to undermine the will and justice of God. The sword was necessary to protect life and prosperity.

Harold then asked whether it would be possible to paint a portrait of a person who held the dove with both hands. The young artist thought a long time. He then said, "I would have to paint a picture of Jesus." For many Muslims Jesus represents an ideal person and ethic. Born of a virgin, prophet from his youth, a word from God or a spirit from God, says the Qur'an. Furthermore, for some Muslims Jesus is the author of the Sermon on the Mount. "Love your enemies, pray for those who persecute you" (Matt. 5:44). This, for many Muslims, is lofty idealism, admirable but not practical in the real world.

How do we as Christians witness within our interfaith relationships to the Jesus who carries a dove with two hands? How do we participate in a kingdom led by a leader who says, "Pray for your enemies" (Matt. 5:44) and "Carry the occupying soliders' pack for twice the legal requirement" (Matt. 5:41)? Most of the world outside the Christian community has never seen anyone witnessing to such a Christ. Crosses led the crusades into butchering of Jews, Muslims and even foreign Christians; the British Empire conquered a world under the sign of a national flag marked by a cross; Middle Eastern Muslims encounter a Western Christianity that carries overwhelming military force in two hands. The U.S. State Department warns that the U.S. will protect its missionaries. How do Muslims of the Middle East meet the real Jesus when he is seen carrying an American flag?

The Gospel of John witnesses to the Jesus with a dove in two hands. In John 6, after the feeding of five thousand, Jesus is aware that the crowd desires to make him a military revolutionary leader, a king. Jesus lived in revolutionary times; others had visions and would arise after Jesus to the challenge to fight Rome. Jesus had another vision, a vision realized through trust, compassion, and humble servanthood.

Jesus represented a new way of being in the world, as he said to Pilate—a kingdom of a different order, in the world but not of the world. On his last night with his disciples, he took off his outer garments and, half naked, washed his disciples' feet. How do we become a Jesus movement that does not believe that authentic power comes out of the barrel of a gun? How do we portray an authentic image of the crucified shepherd who carries a dove with two hands and whose love draws people to the cross?

It is this Jesus who is the Way, the Truth and the Life. It is this Jesus who says, Walk my way, in my truth and light. It is this Jesus who has the capacity to cross and permeate walls and boundaries, for this Jesus embodies the power that holds galaxies and embraces enemies.

Sermon 2
## The "Among-the-Gentiles" God
Text: Matthew 2:1-12

Epiphany is a major celebration of the shining forth of the light and life of the glory of God. The wise men from the East, the world of Gentiles, arrive to present royal gifts to a future King of the Jews. The story of the wise men is the story of the "among-the-Gentiles" God. The wise men are powerful witnesses to what the Gospel of John describes as "the true light which enlightens everyone coming into the world" (John 1:9). It is this same light that was made concrete, fully incarnate in Jesus.

Matthew, like John, sees the coming of Jesus as having its origin in the realm of the divine. Wise men were thinkers, philosophers who believed that the movement of cosmic forces seen in the stars determined the world of history. They sought the meaning of life, and a new star was a sign of hope. A star in this particular quadrant was a sign that a king had been born in Judea who perhaps had the power to transform life even beyond the Judean borders. These are seekers of truth and life among the Gentiles. They follow the star and bring gifts to the king. They refuse to be part of a despotic king's plot. They are signs of the God loose among the Gentiles.

About forty-five years ago, I, along with my wife, Mary Lou, and our three-year-old son, Mark, were sent to a small village in northern Nigeria named Lamurde. We were to start a new Lutheran Seminary where young men would be trained for the ministry. Shortly after moving into our new world we began to hear of a traditional medicine doctor named Malam Hankuri (Sir Patience). People came from miles around, even from Southern Nigeria, to be healed by a humble, quiet human being who had the marvelous gift of healing people's bodies and minds. The marvels of traditional healing had been passed on to him by his father. Leaves, herbs and wisdom were the secrets to his healing power.

One day in the rainy season, when the roads were impassable, a young man was carried to our small medical clinic. He had fallen from a tree and had broken the femur in his leg. The bone protruded from his thigh. I had no idea how we could help this young man. A student said, "We will take him to Malam Hankuri." Malam Hankuri set the leg bone and applied leaves to the open wound. A few weeks later, when the roads were better, a Danish medical doctor stopped to check on our small medical dispensary. I asked him to check the young man's leg. He reported that the leg had been set perfectly and the wound had healed with no sign of infection. Dr. Faartoft told me that he knew Dr. Hankuri and frequently sent persons who had psychological problems to him for his healing touch. Malam Hankuri had a sliding scale for his treatment. The very poor paid little or nothing, and the wealthy paid much more. Malam Hankuri had listened to the story of Jesus and been attracted by the message. However, he never became a member of the church. It was known that he had six wives who were the nurses and caretakers of his many patients. He would not send five of his wives away, as dictated by the church, and destroy the healing work that had been given him.

I was always convinced that the Wisdom, the Logos of God that enlightens every human and became concrete in Jesus, was powerfully at work in his life. Tragically, while undergoing surgery needed to save his life, he died in Dr. Faartoft's hospital—a "God-among-the-Gentiles" saint.

As Christians we have not always recognized the Wisdom/Word of God that enlightens everyone coming into the world. We see it even in the designations given to the visitors from the East. They are sometimes called magicians or sorcerers, words that imply that they are closer to demons than to

God, Light, Life and Truth. Traditional healers like Malam Hankuri have often been called "witch" doctors.

The Bible contains a variety of traditions. There are hate-the-enemy traditions and an-eye-for-an-eye traditions. Deuteronomy 13 expresses a "burn all pagan Gentile men, women and children as a burnt offering to God" tradition. Jesus rejects these traditions. "You have heard love your neighbor and hate your enemy, but I say to you love your enemy, [even your Gentile enemies,] pray for those who persecute you" (Matt. 5:44).

In the Hebrew Scriptures, Jonah grounds that love of the Gentile enemy in the love of God. Jonah was called by God to preach to the Assyrian Empire, centered in Nineveh, the terrorist power of the 9th and 8th centuries B.C.E. Cities that rebelled against this despotic power faced death. Every male lost his head, and skulls were piled by the city gate.

Jonah refused the call and took flight in the opposite direction. Is he terrorized by the evil empire? No. He is terror-ized by the grace of God! Jonah finally is convinced to go to Nineveh. He preaches. The terrorists repent. Jonah fumes at the forgiveness of God: "I knew you were a God of love and forgiveness. Your embrace of the enemy is more than I can tolerate." How often do we hear that attitude expressed in the insanity of our own war-crazed society?

This inclusive biblical tradition not only announces God's love for the whole of humanity. It announced the God active among the Gentiles, the God who inspired the Gentiles to seek meaning in their lives, to search the heavens and be led to the King. In scripture there are numerous God-among-the-Gentiles people.

Melchizidek, the unknown Canaanite King of Righteous-ness, blessed Abraham, the father of faith. From outside the household of faith comes a blessing of God.

Jesus was part of that tradition. Jesus saw God every-where. God was in creation. Jesus' most radical statement, "love your enemy," was not grounded in Torah, the prophets; it was embedded in creation. God's love fell as rain and created life through the sunshine. Life was poured out upon the good and the evil. Jesus saw God alive in the Gentile widow who fed Elijah the prophet, in the Gentile Naaman who was healed by Elisha, and in the Gentile Samaritan leper who came back to give thanks for his healing. In portraying compassion Jesus tells a story of the Samaritan heretic who stopped to save the beaten traveler on the Jericho Road. For Jesus, God was loose among the Gentiles.

A number of years ago, I was visiting Cairo. One afternoon Vogelaar took me to visit a number of mosques. At the end of the afternoon we visited an elderly imam, and through Vogelaar I was able to have a wonderful conversation with him. I imagined him leading prayers several times a day. He would begin standing within the awesome presence of God. Muslims have ninety-nine names for God, including the Most Gracious, the Most Merciful, and the Master of the Day of Judgment. However, Allah is beyond all names and transcends all human attempts to point to the awesome wonder. Muslims proclaim "Allah Achbar" (Allah is greater than all of that). Then, leading the community, he would kneel and eventually place his forehead on his prayer mat on the ground signifying that he and the community surrendered their total lives to Allah.

I asked this gentle man how he would spend his days. He said that he would visit his people who lived around the mosque. Many were very poor and struggled to have food for their families. Others were very wealthy. The Imam said that he spent many hours trying to request money from the rich to enable the poor to eat. He said one of the most difficult tasks was to get the wealthy to open their fists that clutched their wealth so it might be shared with the hungry. The Imam then said that he gave a great deal of time to the youth. There was always hope in youth, he said. However, he described the crisis that was developing among the youth in the areas of integrity and morality. He said that imported tapes and videos from the U.S. spewed out violence and sexual exploitation among his people. It was difficult to combat this secular invasion from the West. Then I asked the old gentleman what he would preach about on Friday, the day of the weekly sermon. He replied that he always sought to find in the Qur'an a passage of comfort. People living in a world of disintegrating security and moral values needed to be comforted.

As we left the mosque, the Imam asked us to have our Christian sisters and brothers pray for his brother-in-law who was very ill. There was no doubt in my mind that God was in the old Imam's life. He was an authentic God-among-the-Gentiles person. I have wondered whether he would be attracted to the story of Jesus. I am quite sure that he would. However, would he ever consider joining a Christian church? Almost certainly he would not. Over 1,000 years of tension and hostility between Muslims and Christians would make that unlikely. The savage treatment of Palestinian Muslims by the Zionists of Israel supported by the United States considered to be Christian in itself, would make it impossible. The Jesus who embodied an all-embracing, forgiving, vulnerable love crucified on a cross is not the Christ reflected in much of Western Christianity. The cross rather symbolizes the power, weapons and destructive power of Western crusaders and imperialists. The God of galaxies in flesh and cross has been lost behind Western Christendom's military and economic power as well as theological orthodoxy.

The among-the-Gentiles God, however, is loose in the world, and the Jesus of the cross continually speaks outside the institutional church as well as through it. There are millions of persons who have been drawn by their own stars to the manger and cross of Jesus and returned to their own communities with their own witness to the God of galaxies particularized in flesh and cross.  Listen to this confession of faith:

> What then does Jesus mean to me? To me he was one of the greatest teachers humanity has ever had. To his believers, he was God's only begotten Son. Could the fact that I do or do not accept this belief make Jesus any more or less an influence in my life? Is all the grandeur of his teaching and doctrine to be forbidden to me? I cannot believe so. To me it implies a spiritual birth. My interpretation, in other words, is that in Jesus' own life is the key to the nearness of God: that he expressed as no other could the spirit and will of God. It is in this sense that I see him and recognize him as the Son of God.[153]

This confession comes from the renowned Indian philosopher, religious and political leader, M. K. Gandhi, who was a Hindu God-among-the-Gentiles saint.

# End Notes

## Introduction

[1] Ignacio Ellacuria, "The Crucified People," *Fundamental Concepts of Liberation Theology*, ed. Ignacio Ellacuria and Jon Sobrino (Maryknoll, NY: Orbis Books, 1993), 580-603. Originally published in Mexico, in *Mysterium Liberationis* (1978).

[2] C. S. Song, *The Scandal of the Crucified World: Perspectives on the Cross and Suffering*, ed. Yacob Tesfai, chapter 10 (Maryknoll, N.Y.: Orbis Books, 1994).

[3] For two examples of this theme see "The Freedom of a Christian (1518)" in *Martin Luther's Basic Theological Writings*, ed. Timothy F. Lull (Minneapolis: Fortress Press, 1989), 30-49, or in *Luther's Works* (LW) 31, *Career of the Reformer I* (Philadelphia: Muhlenberg Press, 1957), 39-58; also "Preface to the Epistle of St. Paul to the Romans" in LW 35, *Word and Sacraments* (Philadelphia: Muhlenberg Press, 1960), 365-80.

[4] *Augsburg Confession, VII.*

[5] Ingemar Oberg finds this dimension of mission in Luther's "Heerpredigt wider den Turken" in *Dr. Martin Luther's Werke, Weimar Edition* (WA), Vol. 30, Part 2, No. 1, 192-194. Oberg's observations are found in the forthcoming translation of his book, *Luther and World Mission: Historical and Systematic Studies with Special Reference to Bible Exposition*, tr. Dean M. Apel (St. Louis: Concordia Publishing House, in press).

[6] Luther's comments appear in an exposition of Psalm 82:4 and are found in LW 13, *Selected Psalms II* (St. Louis: Concordia Publishing House, 1955), 64-65.

[7] See "Sermon on Auffahrttage (May 22, 1522)" in *Dr. Martin Luther's Werke, Weimar Edition*, Vol. 10, Dritte Abteilung, p. 140.

[8] An excellent discussion of this topic is found in Mark Gibbs and T. Ralph Morton, *God's Frozen People* (Philadelphia: Westminster Press, 1964).

[9] See WA 39.I, p. 454, line 4ff.; also LW 25, *Lectures on Romans* (St. Louis: Concordia Publishing House, 1972), see exposition on Romans 2:15.

[10] The phrase "finitum capax infiniti" does not actually occur in the Marburg Articles or Colloquy but in time became a summary of the Lutheran position. For an example, see Paul Tillich, *The History of Christian Thought*, ed. Carl Braaten (New York and Evanston: Harper and Row, Publishers, 1968), 262.

[11] "To the Christian Nobility," LW 44, *The Christian in Society I* (Philadelphia: Fortress Press, 1966), 13.

[12] H. Butterfield, *Christianity and History* (New York: Charles Scribner's Sons, 1950), 146.

[13] "The Heidelberg Disputation (1518)" in Lull's collection (see Note 3), 30-49; also in LW 31: 39-58.

[14] In chapter 2 we will return for a further discussion of Luther's theology of the cross.

## Chapter 1

[15] Jon Sobrino, *Jesus the Liberator: A Historical Theological View, Part IV* (Maryknoll, NY: Orbis Books, 1999), 195-271. See also Leonardo Boff, *Way of the Cross—Way of Justice* (Maryknoll, NY: Orbis Books, 1982). Boff wrote this meditation after six major publications dealing with Christology. See also Walter Altmann, *Luther and Liberation: A Latin American Perspective* (Minneapolis: Fortress Press, 1992).

[16] See Joanne Carlson Brown and Rebecca Parker, "For God So Loved the World," in *Christianity, Patriarchy and Abuse: A Feminist Critique*, ed. J. C. Brown and Carole R. Bohn (Cleveland, OH: The Pilgrim Press, 1989), 1-30.

[17] See "A Meditation on Christ's Passion" in Lull's collection, pp. 165-172, particularly 166-167 where Luther speaks of the severe punishment of the dearest Son. Gustaf Aulén argues that this theme in Luther is subordinate to the theme of God's victory over sin, death and the devil in *Christus Victor: An Historical Study of the Three Types of the Idea of the Atonement* (New York: Collier Books, Macmillan Publishing Co., 1969).

[18] Kosuke Koyama, "The Wrath of God in a Culture of Tranquility," *Water Buffalo Theology* (Maryknoll, NY: Orbis Books, 1998 ), 68.

[19] In particular, Lutheran Orthodoxy has had a tendency to minimize the role of evil in speaking of human suffering and to dramatize the role of God's judgment. One might call this the demonization of God within orthodoxy. For another interpretation of this theme see *The Scandal of a Crucified World: Perspectives on the Cross and Suffering*, ed. Yacob Tesfai (Maryknoll, NY: Orbis Books, 1994); particularly note chapters 1 (Tesfai) and 10 (C. S. Song).

[20] Terrence E. Fretheim has written brilliantly on the theme of the suffering of God in the Old Testament. See *The Suffering of God: An Old Testament Perspective* (Philadelphia: Fortress Press, 1984). In a recent article Fretheim has used this theme in developing a Christology. See "Christology and the Old Testament," in *Who Do You Say I Am?* ed. Mark Allen Powell and David Bauer (Louisville: Westminster John Knox Press, 1999), particularly p. 212. Fretheim's work is indebted to Abraham Heschel, *The Prophets* (New York: Harper and Row, 1962).

[21] Choan-Seng Song, *Third Eye Theology*, revised ed. (Maryknoll, NY: Orbis Books, 1979), 83-88.

[22] Quoted by James Cone in "An African-American Perspective on the Cross and Suffering," in *The Scandal of the Crucified World: Perspectives on the Cross and Suffering*, ed. Yacob Tesfai (Maryknoll, NY: Orbis Books, 1994), 59.

[23] Arvind P. Nimal, "Doing Theology from a Dalit Perspective," in *A Reader in Dalit Theology*, ed. A. P. Nimal (Madras/Gurukul, 1990).

[24] *Voices of Women: An Asian Anthology*, ed. Alison O'Grady (Singapore: Asian Christian Women's Conference, 1978).

[25] Dietrich Bonhoeffer, *Letters and Papers from Prison*, enlarged edition, ed.

Eberhard Bethge (New York: Collier Books, Macmillan Publishing Co., 1971), 361.

26 Aulen, *Christus Victor: An Historical Study of the Three Types of the Idea of the Atonement.*

27 For similar thoughts see Douglas John Hall, *God and Human Suffering: An Exercise in the Theology of the Cross* (Minneapolis, Augsburg Publishing House. 1986), 93-121.

28 John Howard Yoder, *The Politics of Jesus: Vicit Agnus Noster* (Grand Rapids: Eerdmans, 1972).

29 See George Forell's discussion of the Council of Arles (318 CE) where Christian soldiers are threatened with excommunication for throwing "down their weapons even in times of peace." *History of Christian Ethics,* Vol. 1 (Minneapolis: Augsburg Publishing, 1979), pp. 58-60.

30 "The Temporal Authority," LW 45:96.

31 Heinrich Bornkamm, *Luther's Doctrine of the Two Kingdoms* (Philadelphia: Fortress Press, 1966).

32 This is called a "just war" ethical possibility. For example, see the collection of essays distributed by *The Christian Century* entitled *War as Crucifixion.*

33 Vítor Westhelle, "The Way the World Ends: An Essay on Cross and Christology," *Currents in Theology and Mission* 27:2 (April 2000), 85-97.

34 Kato Kitamori, *The Theology of the Pain of God* (Richmond: John Knox Press, 1965), 119-121.

35 Douglas John Hall, *God and Human Suffering,* 98, 113.

36 Jürgen Moltmann, *The Crucified God: The Cross of Christ as the Foundation and Criticism of Christian Theology* (New York: Harper and Row, 1974), 235-249, particularly 248.

37 Elizabeth Johnson, *She Who Is: The Mystery of God in Feminine Theological Discourse* (New York: Crossroads, 1992), 270-271.

38 Sobrino, op. cit., p. 231. In *Jesus the Liberator* Sobrino uses the analogy of a mother, who loves her oppressed people, allowing her son to be sent into battle for the sake of the future of her people.

39 Justin Martyr, *Apology* I:46, II:13; Clement of Alexandria, *The Stomata,* Book I, chapters 4 and 5; Augustine, *The Retroactions,* Book I, chapter 12, section 3.

40 Quoted by Jan Bonda in *The One Purpose of God: An Answer to the Question of Eternal Punishment* (Grand Rapids: William B. Eerdmans Publishing Company, 1993). Bonda also notes similar views in Clement of Alexandria and Gregory of Nyssa (pp. 34-44).

41 Jacques Dupuis, *Towards a Christian Theology of Religious Pluralism* (Maryknoll, NY: Orbis Books, 1997), chapters 3-5, pp. 84-157.

42 See Wolfhart Pannenberg, "The Religions from the Perspective of Christian Theology and the Self-Interpretation of Christianity in Relation to Non-Christian Religions," *Modern Theology* 9:3 (July 1993), 285-297, particularly 293. See also Carl Braaten, "The Universal Meaning of Jesus Christ," *LCA Partners* (December 1980), 13-16.

43 Debates have been held over whether a Christology is expressive or constitutive of the reality of God. I believe this either/or needs to be countered with a healthy Lutheran both/and. On the one hand the Cosmic Abba comes to expression in Jesus' mission, crucifixion and resurrection; on the other, that "coming to expression" takes concrete form as the Infinite breaks into, fuses with and transforms the finite.

This concretization of the reality of God is then constitutive of God and if so a promise of God's relationship to the whole of inter-stellar reality.

**Chapter 2**

[44] "Justification Today: Studies and Reports." Geneva: LWF Publication, Supplement to No. 1 (1965): 18.

[45] Gerhard O. Forde, *On Being a Theologian of the Cross: Reflections on Luther's Heidelberg Disputation, 1518* (Grand Rapids, MI: Wm. B. Eerdmans Publishing Co., 1997), 81ff.

[46] Ibid., viii ff.

[47] Martin Luther, "The Heidelberg Disputation," in *Luther's Works* 31, ed. Harold J. Grimm and Helmut T. Lohmann (Philadelphia: Muhlenberg Press, 1957), 53.

[48] Forde, *On Being a Theologian of the Cross*, 90.

[49] Ibid., 90.

[50] Ibid., 87.

[51] Luther, "The Heidelberg Disputation," 52-53.

[52] *Martin Luther's Basic Theological Writings*, ed. Timothy F. Lull (Minneapolis: Fortress Press, 1989), 169.

[53] Ibid., 168.

[54] Forde, *On Being a Theologian of the Cross*, 90.

[55] Luther, "The Heidelberg Disputation," 57-58.

[56] Vítor Westhelle, "A Vision: Culling Some Prophetic Thoughts," in *Envisioning a Lutheran Communion: Perspectives for the 21st Century*, ed. Mark Thomsen and Vítor Westhelle (Minneapolis: Kirk House Publishers, 2002), 138.

[57] Valerie Saiving, "The Human Situation: A Feminine Viewpoint," in *Pastoral Psychology* (April 1966), 29-42. Saiving's position was first articulated in 1960.

[58] Forde, *On Being a Theologian of the Cross*, xiii-ix, 84-86.

[59] Ibid., viii.

[60] Ibid. Forde makes a side comment that there are victims and victimization; however, they are of secondary concern. This reality cannot become our preoccupation without obstructing our vision of human guilt.

[61] For an excellent description of the Biblical understanding of the suffering of God see Terence Fretheim, *The Suffering of God: An Old Testament Perspective* (Philadelphia: Fortress Press, 1984).

[62] Elie Wiesel, *Night* (New York: Bantam Books, 1982), 61.

[63] Phil-Ruge Jones in his LSTC Ph.D. dissertation finds in Luther's sermon "The Blessed Sacrament of the Holy and True Body of Christ and the Brotherhoods" the thought of solidarity with the marginalized.

[64] Forde, *On Being a Theologian of the Cross*, x.

[65] Ibid.

[66] Forde, *On Being a Theologian of the Cross*, xi.

[67] Ibid. 83.

[68] Ibid., xi.

[69] Ibid., 84-85.

[70] Ibid., 84.

[71] Ibid. It is unfortunate that Forde does not use this insight to develop a dimension within his own thought that would be similar to that which he is attacking here.

72 Dietrich Bonhoeffer, *Letters and Papers from Prison* (New York: Collier Books, Macmillan Publishing Company, 1972), 367.

73 Forde, *On Being a Theologian of the Cross*, 85, n.16. Forde's recognition of this reality is certainly correct as he affirms that in this sense suffering may be redemption.

74 *Martin Luther: Selections from His Writings*, ed. John Dillenberger (New York: Anchor Books Doubleday, 1962), 226.

75 Ewald M. Plass, *What Luther Says*, III (St. Louis, MO: Concordia Publishing House, 1959): 1550, para. 5037.

76 Ibid., 1558, para. 5064.

77 It should be noted that in *Bondage of the Will* Luther does not rule out human freedom in the realm of civil action.

78 Abraham Lincoln, *Second Inagural Address,* March 4, 1865.

79 Forde, *On Being a Theologian of the Cross*, 49-67.

80 *LW* 33:138-140. See also 36-34, where Luther argues that God's fore-knowledge is grounded in the necessity of God's immutable will. Found also in *Martin Luther: Selections from His Writings*, 190-192.

81 Alister E. McGrath, *Luther's Theology of the Cross* (Grand Rapids, MI: Baker Books, 1985), 165 ff.; Kurt Hendel, lecture in Mark Thomsen's class, "Contextual Theologies of the Cross," LSTC, Spring 2003.

82 Gerhard Forde, "Eleventh Locus, Christian Life, Justification Today," in *Christian Dogmatics*, Vol 2, ed. Carl Braaten and Robert Jensen (Philadelphia: Fortress Press, 1984), 468.

**Chapter 3**

83 An excellent source of statistics is found in *World Christian Encyclopedia*, 2nd ed., Vol. I, ed. David B. Barrett, George T. Kurian and Todd M. Johnson (Oxford University Press, 2000).

84 Peter Berger, *The Sacred Canopy* (New York: Anchor Books, 1969), Chapter 1.

85 The Amsterdam Declaration, no. 6.

86 Ibid., no. 5.

87 Karl Rahner, "Christianity and the Non-Christian Religions," in *Christianity and Other Religions*, ed. John Hick and Brian Hebbelthwaite (Philadelphia: Fortress Press, 1981), 63, from Rahner, *Theological Investigations, vol. 5* (New York: Seabury Press, 1966).

88 Ibid. p. 75.

89 Hans Küng, "The World Religions in God's Plan of Salvation," in *Christian Revelation and World Religions*, ed. Joseph Neusner (London: Burns and Oates, 1967), 51ff.

90 *Redemptoris Missio*, paragraph 55, "Dialogue With Our Brothers and Sisters of Other Religions," 1990.

91 *Dominus Iesus VI*, paragraph 22.

92 Kurt Hendel, professor of historical theology at the Lutheran School of Theology in Chicago, makes this statement.

93 Wolfhart Pannenberg, "The Religions from the Perspective of Christian Theology and the Self-Interpretation of Christianity in Relation to Non-Christian Religions," *Modern Theology* 9:3 (July 1993), 285-297.

94 See, e.g., Wolfhart Pannenberg, "Toward a Theology of the History of Religions," *Basic Questions in Theology II* (Philadelphia: Fortress Press, 1971), 65-118; Carl E. Braaten, "The Gospel of Salvation and the World Religions," chapter 4 of *The Flaming Center: A Theology of Christian Mission* (Philadelphia: Fortress Press, 1977), 93-119; Carl E. Braaten,

No Other Gospel: Christianity Among the World Religions (Minneapolis: Fortress Press, 1992), 65-81.

[95] NCC Statement Interfaith Relations and the Churches, section "Jesus Christ and Reconciliation."

[96] Paul F. Knitter, No Other Name? A Critical Survey of Christian Attitudes toward the World Religions (Maryknoll, NY: Orbis Books, 1985).

[97] The Myth of Christian Uniqueness, ed. John Hick and Paul Knitter (Maryknoll, NY: Orbis Books, 1987).

[98] Ibid., viii.

[99] Daniel B. Clendenin, Many Gods, Many Lords: Christianity Encounters World Religions (Grand Rapids, MI: Baker Books, 1995), 31.

[100] Gordon D. Kaufmann, "Religious Diversity, Historical Consciousness, and Christian Theology," in The Myth of Christian Uniqueness, ed. John Hick and Paul F. Knitter (Maryknoll, NY: Orbis Books, 1987), 9.

[101] Knitter, No Other Name? x.

[102] Knitter, No Other Name? xi.

[103] Rosemary R. Reuther, "Feminism and Jewish Christian Dialog," in The Myth of Christian Uniqueness, ed. Hick and Knitter, 141.

[104] Christian Uniqueness Reconsidered: The Myth of a Pluralistic Theology of Religions, ed. Gavin D'Costa (Maryknoll, NY: Orbis Books), xxii.

[105] John B. Cobb, "Beyond Pluralism," and J. A. DiNoia, "Pluralist Theology of Religions," in Christian Uniqueness Reconsidered: The Myth of a Pluralistic Theology of Religions, ed. Gavin D'Costa, 81ff. and 119ff.

[106] DiNoia, "Pluralist Theology of Religions," 119-34; Surin, "A 'Politics of Speech': Religious Pluralism in the Age of McDonald's Hamburgers," in Christian Uniqueness Reconsidered, ed. D'Costa, 192 ff.

[107] M. M. Thomas, "A Christ-Centered Humanist Approach to Religions in the Indian Pluralistic Context," in Christian Uniqueness Reconsidered, ed. D'Costa, 49ff.

[108] Mark Thomsen, The Word and the Way of the Cross: Christian Witness among Muslim and Buddhist People (Chicago: The Evangelical Lutheran Church in America, Division for Global Mission, 1993).

[109] Gilkey, "Plurality and Its Implications," in The Myth of Christian Uniqueness, ed. Hick and Knitter, 44-45.

[110] The Uniqueness of Jesus: A Dialogue with Paul Knitter, ed. Leonard Swidler and Paul Mojzes (Maryknoll, NY: Orbis Books, 1997); Paul F. Knitter, Jesus and the Other Names (Maryknoll, NY: Orbis Books, 1996); Paul F. Knitter, One Earth Many Religions (Maryknoll, NY: Orbis Books, 1995).

[111] Knitter, One Earth Many Religions, 181.

[112] Knitter, Jesus and the Other Names, 10-11, where Knitter describes his life experiences that moved him to take justice issues seriously.

[113] Ibid., 17-19.

[114] Ibid., 19.

[115] Ibid., 23.

[116] The Uniqueness of Jesus: A Dialogue with Paul Knitter, ed. Swidler and Mojzes, 152-54.

[117] Knitter, Jesus and the Other Names, 73-83, and The Uniqueness of Jesus, 7-11, 155-161.

[118] Knitter, Jesus and the Other Names, 79.

[119] The Uniqueness of Jesus, 182. It probably should be noted that the pluralists John Hick and Raimon Panniker think that Knitter has

conceded too much to his critics. See Hick, "Five Misgivings," 79ff., and Panniker, "Whose Uniqueness?" 111ff. in this same volume.

120 *The Uniqueness of Jesus*, 155.

121 Ibid., 14-15 n. 20; 155ff.

122 Ibid., 157 n. 5; 158.

123 Ibid., 11.

124 Ibid., 13.

125 S. Mark Heim, *Salvation:Truth and Difference in Religion*,(Maryknoll, NY: Orbis Books), 101-10.

126 Ibid., 214.

127 Ibid., 224.

128 Ibid., 124.

129 Ibid., 133-136.

130 Ibid., 145.

131 Ibid., 215.

132 Ibid., 149.

133 Ibid., 177.

134 Ibid., 160.

135 Ibid., 167.

136 Ibid., 217.

137 Ibid., 215.

138 For an evaluation of Heim from a Catholic perspective see Jacques Dupuis, *Toward a Christian Theology of Religious Pluralism* (Maryknoll, NY: Orbis Books, 1997).

## Chapter 4

139 The resurrection faith lies behind the theology of the cross found in this document, but the focus of this essay is the significance of the cross for our faith and mission.

140 Carl Braaten, *The Apostolic Imperative* (Minneapolis: Augsburg, 1985), 75.

141 Wesley Ariarajah, *The Bible and People of Other Faiths* (Geneva: World Council of Churches, 1985), 70.

142 John. B. Cobb, Jr., *Beyond Dialog: Toward a Mutual Transformation of Christianity and Buddhism* (Philadelphia: Fortress Press, 1982).

143 Anselm, *Proslogion*, Chapter III.

144 Blaise Pascal, *Pascal's Thoughts*, in *The Harvard Classics*, ed. Charles Eliot, 48:83-87 (Section III, paragraph 233) (New York: P. F. Collier and Son, 1910).

## Chapter 5

145 Robert Schreiter, *The New Catholicity* (Maryknoll, NY: Orbis Books, 1997), 1-14.

146 George Tinker, *Missionary Conquest: The Gospel and Native American Cultural Genocide,* (Minneapolis: Fortress Press, 1993), 36.

147 Marc H. Ellis, *Unholy Alliance: Religion and Atrocity in Our Time* (Minneapolis: Fortress Press, 1997).

148 John Pobee, Research Report 16: *The Worship of the Free Market and the Death of the Poor* (Uppsala: Life and Peace Institute, 1994), 31.

149 Hunger facts are available on the Bread for the World Web site: http://www.bread.org/hungerbasics.

150 Michael Welker, *God the Spirit* (Minneapolis: Fortress Press, 1994), 17.

151 Jonathan Kozol, *Savage Inequality* (New York: Harper Collins, 1992).

152 An excellent source of statistics is found in *World Christian Encyclopedia*, *vol. I*, 2nd edition, ed. David B. Barrett, George T. Kurian, and Todd M. Johnson (Oxford University Press, 2001).

**Chapter 6**

153 M. K. Gandhi, *qb*, compiled by R. K. Prabhu (Ahmedabad: Navajivan Publishing, 1959), 4.